The Observer

WILD TWIN

upwards to unknown galaxies,

GHOST

This book is for Dad, Cyril Young, 1931 – 2023

And for Amy and Pearl, as ever.

We sang of the future
We'd celebrate the past
Now memory is the theatre
The ghost light goes out last.

from 'Ghost Light',
by John Canning Yates / A. P. Yates

Published by Little Toller Books in 2024
Ford, Pineapple Lane, Dorset

Typeset in Garamond by Little Toller Books

Printed in Cornwall by TJ Books

All papers used by Little Toller Books are natural, recyclable products made from wood grown in sustainable, well-managed forests

A catalogue record for this book is available from the British Library

ISBN 978-1-915068-40-8

WILD
TWIN
JEFF YOUNG

LITTLE TOLLER

Contents

*When everything changed and people had died
and I felt like I was dying too, I began to dream of
places I had been to and could no longer go. And so
I went to where I always go, into the shadowplay of
memory where I might find an echo, a reflection,
the wild twin that always runs on ahead over the
edge, into the beyond. The part of me that wants to
disappear, to become mist, invisible, to be elsewhere.*

*My mother loved to tell the story of how, when
visiting other people's homes, my chosen chair was
usually the one nearest the door. I would sit there,
wearing my coat, ready to leave at the earliest
opportunity, wanting to escape. I still sit in that
chair, ready to slip away to a place where no one
can see me, where I can vanish into darkness, be
invisible, a shadow, or the becoming of a shadow,
where I can become my wild twin.*

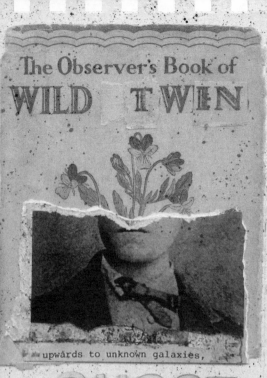

The Observer's Book of
WILD TWIN

upwards to unknown galaxies,

GHOST

becomes a bird again.

INVISIBL

Amsterdam. Kolkje

falling through space,

WILL'S CIGARETTES.

HOME

MEMORY

Part One

Worse than not realising the dreams of your youth
would be to have been young and never dreamed at all.

Jean Genet

Wild Twin

There are horses and angels and a broken bird in a shoebox nest. Soon it will be daylight, and my dad will come home from the printing factory nightshift. I don't want him to come home, or rather when he does come home, I want to be invisible.

My dad is a kind and gentle soul with pale blue eyes. Sometimes they remind me of winter. Grey rather than blue, a degree too close to ice to enter. I have often found it difficult to look into those eyes, and today will be more difficult than ever. It's not because of him or his eyes that I want to be invisible. I have always felt that way. The dream of disappearing.

It's seven o'clock on a Monday morning in March, sometime in the 1970s, and I'm not going to work. In fact, I'm never going there again because I never wanted to work there in the first place. Once, an airship circled the building, and the world was strange and beautiful for a few hours. Another time, a ladybird plague turned the walkways into an architecture of insects. On the day a princess came to open the building, gardeners came in lorries to decorate the streets with thousands of flowers and the city became a garden. The rest of the time this office block was a deathly place, where men disintegrated before your eyes and drowned their misery in endless cups of vending machine hot chocolate and drunken lunchtimes. There was the man who drank oxtail soup while he read the Bible, using a nasal inhaler to stir his brew. There was the man who went for three-hour, five-pints-of-bitter lunches, forcing himself to vomit in the toilet cubicle before resuming work. There was also the receptionist who wrote the words *Zoological Starfucker* in a ledger of planning applications, and never explained their meaning. The valuation officer who answered every question with either *Tickety-boo* or *Deary fuck...* The main function of the department I worked in seemed to be buying up derelict buildings and demolishing them, to make way for traffic widening schemes, to kill the city and replace it with roads. My job was to collect document folders from the desks of men, put them in filing cabinets, deliver more documents to more desks, and then collect the folders again later and put them back in filing cabinets. I also refilled the photocopier with paper. And broke the photocopier. That was more or less my job. The dole sent me. I thought the council would reject me, but they took me on the spot and told me it was a job for life. I didn't want the job for life.

One Friday evening in March I clock off early, go to the pub, have a few beers, and decide I'm never going back. I've decided this before, but I never had the courage to leave, and would always be back at my desk on Monday morning. Not this time. I've made up my mind. When Monday comes, I'm going to disappear. I'm going to Paris.

On Saturday I buy a book – the wrong book – for the road: *The Mote in God's Eye* by Larry Niven, because I want a book that lasts for months and keeps me safe in an imaginary world. Then I drink with friends in the Shakespeare, and we go up onto the aerial walkway, Shankland's amputated pavements in the sky, and rub sulphate into our gums. It turns out to be paracetamol crushed to dust. We head to a Chinese restaurant infested with cockroaches and eat egg foo young in a cellar. Later, I watch the boxer Alan Rudkin propping up the bar in the Globe and I study the scars around his eyes. I try to speak to him, but he likes to stand in silence, drink until he's unsteady on his feet, and walk home alone in the dark. One day in the future he will be found in the street, dead, alone as he always seems to be. A champion fighter's end in night and rain.

I spend the weekend thinking about what I'm about to do, the thing I haven't told my parents I'm going to do. On Sunday morning my friend Stan phones and says he's coming with me. It's been on and off, and now it's on. I sit in my bedroom, curtains closed, in the dark, frightened, listening to records – Can's *Tago Mago*, Eno's *Taking Tiger Mountain*, Funkadelic's *Maggot Brain* and John Cale's *Paris 1919*, which I decide is the greatest record ever made; Robert Wyatt's *Rock Bottom* and *Ruth is Stranger Than Richard*, the melancholy slumber of his music, that fragile yearning voice submerged in shadow and water. I sit in my bedroom reading poems, too – Gregory Corso's *Bomb*, Anna Kavan's *Ice* (my current obsession), listening to Luke Kelly and reading Brendan Behan, always looking for signals, codes. Into the half-dead hours, into the restless sleep in my small bedroom full of books and records and the secret stash of Lebanese Red in the drawer beneath the bed. I look at maps and read about Paris, about Julian Green's Paris where, *the more astonishing it seemed... that so vast a city could fit into so short a name...* And then when Monday comes, I get up at 7am to hitchhike to my imagined Paris of water lilies, bridges, absinthe, delinquent poets and the graveyard shrines of painters and rock stars.

Downstairs, our home is a cabinet of curiosities curated by my mother. I sit here in our living room in the shadows looking at the nick-nacks on the shelves and the display cabinet full of ornaments, a magical system of memory. This is where the angels live, a host of tiny angels, grouped in a circle like a white ceramic choir. On the walls there are horses, reproduction paintings picked up in auction sales. In a shoebox on the window shelf a broken-winged bird sleeps in a heap of handkerchiefs and woollen gloves, a nest of ladies' accessories. Once again, Mum has rescued a wounded blackbird and is feeding it with an eye dropper, hoping to give it a second chance at life. I make memories for the future. I absorb the atmosphere of the room until I become the room.

Almost fifty years later, when I sit in this same room, I will look at the same ornaments and objects and they will be talismans pulling me into the past, time travel codes and mechanisms. On a shelf there is a small wooden jar that smells of camphor. When I inhale its aroma, I go back to the days of my childhood. Camphor and creosote and a memory of Dad painting the garden fence. On the stairs there is a framed drawing of a Parisian street scene, a naïve, biro sketch of strollers on the banks of the Seine, a pom pom poodle, an accordion player, like something you'd doodle on a napkin. But it works as an entry point into an imaginary city. The shadows on the stairs become Paris, become Henry Miller's fleas in the Villa Borghese, become *Alphaville* and *400 Blows* and water lilies, and strangers who are angels in disguise.

I've dreamed about it and read the books, every book I could get my hands on that says 'Paris', that smells of 'Paris', and I want to live in the dream of it and I want the pages of it to come to life and become actual streets I can walk down. And I want to be a beatnik drifter, so I'm wearing the boots and the shirt a hitchhiker would wear – I know, because I've read Jack Kerouac. I've packed my army surplus duffle bag with a penknife, a brand-new passport and a map and my bundled-up anxieties and here I am, in the family living room, ready to go into the great adventure, in my jeans and Kerouac lumberjack shirt, in the memory of the morning where the ornaments and flower paintings and family photographs play their part in the dawning moment. There's a pile of old comics next to the sofa, mostly Laurel and Hardy comics I picked up in the market, which I like to read before I go to work, which somehow give me comfort and protect me from the misery of the day ahead, in the job I hate, in the life I don't want to live inside. I sit reading a Stan and Ollie adventure until my dad comes in from the factory nightshift, wearing his blue overalls, sensing something different about the day. I know he's going to say it before he says it, quietly, as he screwdrivers the lid off a tin of Swarfega and dips his fingers in. 'Not going to work then?' And I reply, quietly, 'No. I'm... I'm hitchhiking. To Paris.' The quiet man, true to his character, slowly shakes his head as he massages his Swarfega oiled fingers to remove the dirt of work. And then he says, very quietly, 'Well, that's a silly thing to do, isn't it?' The nightshift in his eyes. The eyes I can't look at. He shakes his head slowly, quietly. He cleans machine oil from his finger nails. And then he dries his hands on a rag and rubs his eyes.

In the film version of this moment, Perry Como is singing on the radio, *Magic moments, memories we've been sharing... Magic moments, when two hearts are caring...* Dad sighs, shakes his head, goes slowly, wearily to bed. He says, 'Take care,' and the quietness of the moment is devastating. *Time can't erase the memory of... these magic moments... filled with love...* He's never once raised his voice to me, but this quietness is like shouting. It's the biggest telling off I've ever had in my life. He's right. It's a silly thing to do. But I am going to do it.

So many memories come half erased, pencil drawings on envelopes, faint daubs, trace elements. The memory of this particular morning comes to me like a Super 8 movie solar flare, pock-marked, playing over and over again with the wrong soundtrack. The shadow and light are right, the murmured voices – it's all in place, apart from the song. I've tried for years to get the memory right, to remember what song was playing on the radio. Perry Como singing *Magic Moments* is an imagined memory, an added element to romanticise the scene. It probably didn't happen but it's there now when I watch the memory. It has become the truth even though it's a lie. Why do I play this memory over and over in my head? I think it's the quietness of my dad's disappointment and his incomprehension. Dramatic turning point. I inflicted a small wound in my dad's soul. I have sweetened the regret with sentimental song.

Mum comes downstairs. Usually, she walks around the house singing but today there are no songs. We eat breakfast together. She's wearing pyjamas with a pattern of constellations on them, imaginary Andromeda, Milky Way. The unremarkable things that happen in this room are ongoing, always, a shadow museum of memory and the sweet-light, beautiful ordinary. She says she thinks I'm mad. She doesn't want to stop me. She makes me some cheese sandwiches and wraps them in silver foil. I gather up my things, there are tears in my eyes. I say goodbye. The room is normally light and airy but now, imperceptibly, it is changing, as if the room itself has become nostalgic for happy times that used to happen here, darkening with melancholy, shifting light and time. And in that altered moment, I disappear.

All these years later I still think of my mother, her hands in her apron, the slight shake of her head. My dad, sadly disappointed in me, wanting me to go to work the way I always do, quietly sighing the simple words, *Well, that's a silly thing*, and then going upstairs. I step over the edge. From this moment everything is a beginning, everything is happening for the very first time. I am about to become unsettled. Uprooted. Become anxiety. Become loneliness. Become silence. Become instability. Uncertainty. Waywardness. The desolation angel. I am about to become wild twin.

Desire Paths

I get the train, one stop up the line to Old Roan station where Stan is waiting for me. To my dismay he's wearing cowboy boots as if he's dressed for the wrong road movie. As far as I'm concerned, the film I'm starring in is directed by Wim Wenders. Or perhaps we are Dennis Wilson and Warren Oates in Monte Hellman's *Two-Lane Blacktop*. Stan clearly hasn't given it a single thought. He hasn't even studied the front cover of Neal Cassidy's *The First Third*. Stan is hungry. We wait for the chip shop to open. When the man behind the counter sees our army duffle bags, he asks us where we're shipping out to. I say *Paris,* Stan says *Norway.* It's already going wrong. We give each other a look, a look that says *What the fuck are you talking about?* And then we go and sit in a bus shelter and eat our chips as if it's our final meal. At the motorway, we stick our thumbs out and straight away a car pulls up. Volvo Estate. Our luck is in.

The general rule when hitching in pairs is the one who sits in the passenger seat does all the talking, and the one who sits in the back is the lucky one who gets to sit back and enjoy the ride. Or work through the anxieties. I'm in the passenger seat, but on this occasion Stan and I both lapse into anxious silence while the driver volunteers his delusion that he's Red Adair's right-hand man, and that he's on his way to cap an oil blowout on an offshore oil rig in the North Sea. When strangers meet other strangers, they get to act out fantasies, to invent a version of themselves that make their lives seem stranger, more romantic, more heroic than they really are. Our driver talks about *crude oil spilled* and how John Wayne's film *Hellfighters* isn't particularly accurate. He tells us Red likes to call a burning rig *The Devil's Cigarette Lighter,* and we pretend to laugh like drains. I notice there's a shopping list written on his hand in blue biro. It doesn't look much like a hell-fighter list, more the list of a new dad – baby powder, baby formula, baby food. He smokes our cigarettes, talks about burning oil and smoke blindness, conflagration and fire geysers of crude. We're relieved when he drops us at Burtonwood airbase, and we sit down on a grass verge to eat my mum's cheese sandwiches. Stan removes the cucumber and throws it on the ground. We could be home in half an hour. We've hitched as far as Nowhere.

If becoming invisible is what I want the most – the altered state of disappearing – then it makes no sense to be going on this journey with Stan. If we're following desire paths, the dream journeys we make, the trespassing into territories other than the ones we've always known, then shouldn't we be travelling alone? But there is a kind of solitude here, ever since we've stopped speaking. In the haulage truck that now carries us along the motorway, Stan draws tattoos of snakes on his hands and eats mint imperials. I talk to the driver about meeting Red Adair's right-hand man and the devil's cigarette lighter. By the time we get to London, his agitated silence is vibrating.

We sleep for an hour or two in the doorway of a hi-fi shop on Tottenham Court Road, and then try for a bed in a homeless shelter – they turn us away because we can't prove we're homeless. Stan falls asleep sitting upright on a bench; I am awake listening to the city beyond. Pigeon flutter, cop sirens, howling drunkard, clang and echo of metal shutters, whistling cleaner, Stan snoring. I study his biro tattoos, miasmic mists swirling around a sketch of Doctor Strange. Astro Man, the DC comic hero he dreams of one day writing. I can't even remember how we know each other. He looks like Samuel Beckett's bastard son, hawk-nosed and lanky. He used to keep his nosebleeds in a jam-jar. He always seems to wear the wrong shoes. He idolises Jack Kirby and Italo Calvino. Sometimes he is so pale that he becomes invisible, achieves the state I'm hoping for myself. And then he jerks back into action, disrupts his own invisibility, disturbs the order of the universe. He despises the Catholic faith but still he goes to mass on Sundays. He owns a typewriter and writes strange lyrics about underwater kingdoms and wild girls in pyjamas. He once found a drunk in the gutter and helped him home, where he propped the man up against the bannister – which broke – and the man fell down two floors and nearly died. He listens to the Ohio Players and the Hall & Oates record *Abandoned Luncheonette*, and buys ten Marvel comics every week. He inhales the smell of printers' ink. His favourite meal is curried spaghetti. He dances like a cartoon. He steals LPs from Virgin Records and Woolworths. He is a clown who laughs like a hyena. He wants to be in Roxy Music. He gave me his copy of Tim Buckley's *Happy Sad* and then he said he wished he hadn't. He knows exactly how tall Michael Moorcock is because he once stood next to him in Lewis's department store. We are 'best friends' who quite often don't even enjoy being together. My parents think he's an idiot. Look at us. We haven't got a clue. Our fate is destitution. Failure. I'm expecting violence. I drink the dregs of a bottle of White Horse whisky. It burns the ulcers in my mouth that have erupted since the *taking the sulphate that was really paracetamol and scouring powder* event. We get moved on by the police who ask us if we're schoolboys. In Victoria, we top and tail on a bench until daylight and then we wash in the toilets and decide to jack in hitching and get the train to Dover. We travel there in silence, apart from Stan crunching sugary Love Hearts. I can't remember what I dreamed of when I fell asleep, but I know that sleep was an escape from fear.

★

In Dover, Stan buys brown wrapping paper and Sellotape and posts his cowboy boots back home to Liverpool. I'm watching him, trying to get my head round the absurdity of this moment. We've been awake for hours, he still doesn't speak, we're about to go abroad for the first time in our lives, and he's wrapping up his cowboy boots. Even the man behind the counter in the post office is trying to fathom it out. Stan is oblivious, carefully knotting the parcel string, handing the boots over to the man. We watch the boots go into the delivery sack and it's like saying goodbye to puppies. Stan has clearly tipped over the edge.

On the ferry to Ostend, we look through rain-streaked windows at grey sea. We sit in silence wondering why we're not on the ferry to Calais. We don't know what to do. We haven't yet learned how to travel. We understand the form of moving from here to there, from one place to another, but we don't know what to do when we arrive. And so, when we disembark at Ostend, we walk and we look. We look at Ostend. We then drink dark beers in a bar on the waterfront, a map spread out on the table. I open my copy of *Hitchhikers Guide to Europe* looking for clues but finding none. It doesn't seem to make any sense to have an instruction manual for living rootless lives. And then Stan speaks, 'I don't want to do this.' I reach out and take hold of his hand and say to him that this is what we talked about. He takes his hand away and tells me he is scared, 'I think we should go home.' And then, silence again. I laugh out loud. I drain my glass. I briefly consider hitting him. And then he says he thinks we should have just gone on a package holiday like everybody else. I tell him I'm not going home. And under no circumstances am I going on a fucking package holiday. He asks me if I'll see him off on the ferry back to Dover. We walk to the ferry, he buys his ticket, he waves goodbye, memory in slow motion, and then he's gone. And I'm alone. *So this is what alone is.*

★

It's dark now and I'm frightened. I walk the streets, trying to work out what to do. On the beach, up against a wooden breakwater, I try to sleep, scared of the wind and dark, huddled in a gully. Strange lights, noises, fear of rising tide, voices in shadows scuttle. I must have nodded off, then I'm suddenly wide-eyed, woken by something dropping onto my stomach. And then again, and then again, and I curl myself up into a ball and stare into the dark. Crabs, like an army, coming over the top of the breakwater, enormous crabs, falling down, onto the sand, onto me. Fuck this. Spooked, I walk back into town, try sleeping in the train station but the lights are too bright, walk for ages until I find a pension in a narrow street near the marina, next door to what appears to be a red-light window, a bored woman inside in her underwear, painting her toenails. I get a room, lie awake in bed, tears falling. For months I've thought about EUROPE, about being far away from home. And now I'm in Europe for the first time in my life, all I can think about is Liverpool.

Ghost Town

My dad bought me typewriters – heavy Olivetti machines like iron animals. I would sit at the dinner table hammering out poems and lyrics that would never become songs. We dream, my friends and I, of being tortured artists and poets. We dream of being cult rock stars. We want to be the Great Misunderstood, the Overlooked Savant, the Lost. We want to be the heroin-addled addict without taking the heroin. We want to be the painter-murderer without committing the crime. We are drawn to the romanticism of failure and delinquency. We are Gully Jimson, Lew Welch, Arthur Craven, Tod Hackett. We want to be uncomfortable in our skin, we want to be tormented souls, we want to be conflicted, damaged goods. We're all about avoidance, loitering in margins and shadows. We don't know who we are or what or who we want to be. Unsurprisingly, none of us have girlfriends. We buy secondhand clothes – old overcoats, paratrooper boots. We go and see bands play in pubs and cellars. We sign on and cash our Giro, then we spend it all on records, books, booze, and a five quid deal of Lebanese Red which we buy in the Masonic on Berry Street. We are always looking for the first Modern Lovers album even though it is just a rumour. *Have you got the Modern Lovers LP?* The people in Probe tell us to come back when it's actually been released. We sit in pubs and talk about John Cale and Jean Genet. We are in love with Astrid Proll, the getaway driver for the Baader-Meinhof gang. We trespass in the docks when they're still ruins scheduled for demolition, when Tate Liverpool hasn't even been dreamed of, when the future isn't one of restaurants and fudge shops but of wrecking balls and dynamite. We sit in Yates's Wine Lodge drinking Aussie White and Bismarck Port and flirt with drunk old ladies. We quote lines of dialogue from *Electra Glide in Blue*; we dream of Arizona highways.

I remember all this but alter the memories. I remember the images rather than the meaning. I keep amnesia at bay by stockpiling mental images and storing them in the archive. This is memory on a mangled cassette, faded, decaying, faltering. Sound and vision recordings of things that might have happened. I am the Great Rememberer and yet the memories are full of flaws and errors. Threadbare remembering. It was long ago. It was only yesterday. It happened like this. It never happened.

There's hardly a pavement in the city that doesn't evoke a memory. There's hardly a building – or a space where there used to be a building – that doesn't spark an image from the past. Remembering is archaeology, sifting and recording fragments in the ruins. All my life I have walked through Liverpool, almost every day, and sometimes I'd walk for miles. But I didn't walk through Liverpool for two years while I was shielding from the pandemic. At some point in those two years, my friend Hugh sent me some photographs from the early 1980s, of Hugh and me and other friends – Marty, Pete, Stan – wandering the city. In my head I reenacted those moments when the photographs were taken. In truth, I couldn't remember any of them being taken and hadn't seen Hugh or any of the others for nearly forty years. In my head, I found myself walking through Liverpool with these young men. Guess work, imaginary journeys, time travel into the photographed moment. The bottle of wine on the stone bench, the paperback book in the pocket of my donkey jacket, the black suede winklepickers… this must be 1981.

★

Earlier, sometime in the 1970s, Kirkby town centre, that time we bought Brian Protheroe's 'Pinball', knowing all the words, the kitchen-sink shabby, careworn poetry of the song. And stealing Ian Hunter's first solo album from Woolworths. A secret love for Clifford T. Ward, buying his records from a secondhand market stall, hiding them beneath my coat, discovering years later that I was not alone. Richard Allen Skinhead books, Peter Cave's *Chopper* on the bedroom bookshelf next to Richmal Crompton and Jean Genet. Drinking brown ale in the civic hall car park. Stay behinds in a prefab alehouse. Alsatians on the flat roof barking through barbed wire. Sometimes we just maraud through fields, through pylon hum static, antennae ghost frequencies, derelict warehouses, asbestos in dust motes, gang den in stolen car wreck, burning oil spill torched with Zippo, mud-sunk mopeds, Kwik-Save trolleys in the breached canal, scavenging Betamax tapes from smithereens of bathroom suites in Hangman's Lane fly tips, dead dog in flooded pit weighed down with brick-noose, piano skeleton in burned out church, hymn books and bibles on demolition bonfires, porn mag library in building site watchman's shack, looted sweet and cig kiosk, farm-barn torched by arsonists, industrial beach winter, ice shards and polystyrene, flotsam on grey sea, marine lake chemical rainbow, beautiful in moonlight. Images, fractured, jagged, sound-tracked with Tago Mago, Jobriath, Church of Anthrax, Telstar, Bitches Brew, The Rubettes.

We still haunted the black canal long after it was our truant zone. I still go there now, stretches between bridges, on my way to see my dad in the same semi-detached house I left to hitch to Paris all those years ago. I can see my schoolfriends – see myself – doing wheelies on the cinder path, smell the fag smoke of scruff-bags practising inhaling. And then I can see me and Marty, Hugh, Pete and Stan walking home from canal-side pubs in the dark, in our war-poet overcoats and stolen pint glasses. We are not wounded but we have minor injuries. Secret depressions, nervous breakdown skirmishes, migraine auras. Crushes on Baby Jane Holzer. We're either on the dole or we have dead-end jobs we hate. Sometimes we get a taxi up to a low-rise block on Grove Street. We make the taxi wait while we buy a twenty quid deal and then we drive back into town, our pockets full of weed wrapped in bits of ripped up newspaper. We know all the lyrics on Lou Reed's *Transformer, Coney Island Baby* and *Berlin*. We listen to the children crying on the song *The Kids* and imagine the producer Bob Ezrin telling his children their mother is dead and recording their screams of grief.

I left school with nothing to show for it and went to work on the strawberry farm. There was a boy who weighed the fruit who went to the same school as me, but he left after trying to kill himself in the chemistry lab after being found out for stealing a girl's leather coat and cutting it up to make a bomber jacket. You could see the distress in his eyes, the chaos inside him. He'd had some kind of shooting accident and there were shotgun pellets just under the surface of his skin. He liked to let you touch him, feel the ammo like gravel moving through his body, lodged between bones. Between collar bone and throat there were tiny gravel planets or rosary beads inside him, and once he cut himself open with a penknife and removed a small lead stone, popped it into his mouth and swallowed it, laughing like a mad god, a boy full of lead constellations.

When I look back, I only remember the weirdness of school, and the violence. Watching the so-called Remedial Class digging in the allotments and scattering corn for the chickens – the chickens whose necks they will one day be taught to wring by Sharman the mad gardening teacher. The still baffling school trip to the Boat Show at Earls Court – a group of boys who weren't remotely interested in boats watching Sharman ogling bikini clad lovelies draped over the bows of motorboats. Me, wearing the light brown suedehead suit passed down to me from Cousin David, for which

I'll get detention. All the details – half-inch turnup, buttonholed lapel, side vents, fob pocket, tassel shoes, Ben Sherman button down. First ever bottle of brown ale in the bar, gulping it down fast, straight from the bottle in case Sharman spots us, but then noticing him on the brown and mild in a corner with a fag on the go. And on the train back to Liverpool, him telling us in *great detail* that we're about to pass the railway bridge near Tring where the Great Train Robbery happened, eyes gleaming with excitement, with the vicarious thrill of *being in the vicinity* of a transgressive act. Fifteen boys studying him, getting the measure of him, storing up the evidence for future use. *One day we will use this against you.*

What a fucking mess it was, this charade of education, with Ashby the Geography teacher with his splintered cane – even after corporal punishment was banned. The way he'd twist your sideburns (we called them sideboards) if you so much as looked to left or right, the cane *thwacking* down onto the palm of your hand if you committed the ultimate crime of looking over your shoulder. The livid red Ds scrawled on your exercise book, the targeted hurling of books and board duster at your face. And then – in a lesson about the Yorkshire coal fields – this great hulk of a man in his blazer and Royal Artillery badge crumbled, crumpled into a weeping heap when he recalled his grandfather going down the pit and dying from emphysema after a lifetime at the coal face. *My grandfather died to keep the engines of this country...* unable to finish his sentence, mopping his damp eyes with his pocket hankie, covering his mouth to keep the pain inside. *Ammunition!* We had him. We would use this against him, too, this vulnerability. Except it didn't happen this way. Next lesson he was back to being a sadist and once again we were slapped and battered for glancing left or right, the charade complete. Then there was Tomlinson the PE teacher – swaggering around with his shirt off so everyone could see the brutal surgery scar curving around his body after the removal of his cancerous lung. And Burns the form teacher – picking at the dimple in his chin with a matchstick, trying to remove the blackheads; McVeigh the Domestic Science Teacher, once running through the cookery room with her hair on fire and dousing the flames with wet tea towels while all the lads laughed their heads off. These people were deranged, damaged, dangerous and shouldn't have been allowed anywhere near children. *These people were our teachers…*

What was school for? What was the general direction of travel? What was I working towards? If we were in any way practical, we were being lined up for apprenticeships. If, like me, you were no good at metal work, you were vaguely ushered in the direction of retail work or low-level, white-collar drudgery. I don't remember there being any choice. I don't remember there being any *encouragement.* If I told a teacher I was interested in going to art school, there was never any guidance or advice. There was just *nothing.* When I told the geography teacher I had sent off for information on horticultural college and mumbled something about being interested in forests, there was nothing. At the one and only careers evening, when I said I'd like to travel, the man talked for a bit about the merchant navy, gave me a brochure, found out I was colour blind and took the brochure back. *Nothing.* I left school with the sole ambition of signing on the dole. Secondary education was a completely pointless five-year event. Or rather, non-event. Nothing.

Here I am now, a 66-year-old man. I'm sitting in a room I have sat in at different stages in my life, and I'm watching the child I used to be. When I was a boy, I picked wild watercress in a stream and kept it in a jam-jar in this room until it began to smell. I collected clumps of moss and kept it in a saucer, watered it daily until my mum threw it away. In the airing cupboard, I grew Sea-Monkeys in salt water until the water stank and my mum flushed them down the toilet. I kept two frogs in a Pyrex bowl but felt sorry for them and set them free in the brook at the bottom of our road. I once put a domino in my mouth and kept it there for hours and still don't know why I did this. I invented my own Dream Machine with painted tracing paper and a faulty bedside lamp on a turntable, years before I'd heard of Brion Gysin. I sat watching television with Sellotape on my hair to try and straighten it because boys laughed at my curls. I made a Fireball XL5 out of breakfast cereal packets and burned it in the garden bonfire. I drew pictures of the men who rode fairground dodgems and bus conductors, and I wanted to be like them when I grew up. When Uncle Bert – who wasn't really an uncle – came to tea, he tried to teach me heraldic calligraphy at the dinner table instead of drawing dodgem men and bus conductors. This didn't interest me, but he taught me how to draw the blemished skin of peaches with pastels and I liked rubbing the chalk into paper with my fingertips and watching the drawing becoming bruised fruit before my eyes. The paper was the blank pages of comics that my dad brought home from the printing factory. When I was alone in this room, I put Beach Boys records on the Dansette and sang along to Sloop John B, dancing like I'd never dare to dance in front of other people. In this room, I read a book called *Starbuck Valley Winter* over and over and wanted to hunt pine martens in the snow. These things and other things happened in this room or in the vicinity of this room and added to its atmosphere. And the ticking mantle clock marked the moments as the room tilted into myth.

We also spent a lot of time in a semi-derelict cottage down a back lane on the edge of Kirkby. The boy who lived there boasted of making an intruder dig his own grave in the swamp-garden at gun point. He wore jackets he said were made from the skins of rabbits he'd shot, but they were actually modified fun fur coats from Chelsea Girl. The floors of the cottage were covered in dogshit and there were vandalised stolen cars in the yard. We never saw the woman who lived there – the boy's mother – and we wondered if he'd killed her. And then one day she turned up wearing a plastic skirt and smelling of cigarettes and hair lacquer. She didn't care that we were staring at her, didn't care about the dogshit. We hated going there but we couldn't keep away. We were drawn to its foul atmosphere, the charisma of its malignancy. The cottage was our hideout and there was half a drum kit and guitars, so we'd make a dreadful racket in the middle of nowhere and drink his mother's Liebfraumilch until we were sick. At home, I'd type up a diary on the rattling Olivetti. Angsty fantasies of – I suppose – my alter ego self, the character I would be if I was in a book or film. I wanted to be in a book like Richard Farina's *Been Down So Long It Looks Like Up to Me*, or Emmett Grogan's *Ringolevio* or Nell Dunn's *Up the Junction*. I think I wanted to be enshrined in printers' ink on pages in paperbacks more than I wanted to be the actual me. My typed-up diary was imitation Kerouac, ripped off Knut Hamsun. I'd write poems or lyrics inspired by Bowie's *The Bewley Brothers*. The slur *pretentious* is a badge of pride.

This drab and shabby city, this 1970s abandoned playground, this ghost town. We don't really notice the boarded-up shops on Bold Street, the four or five restaurants that we never go to, the dereliction, dirt. When my mum was a child, Bold Street was considered to be so exclusive that she was afraid (and wasn't allowed) to go there. On a recent walk along the street, I counted fifty-eight eating places, Bold Street literally eating itself alive.

We used to follow desire paths, out beyond the city, walking for miles along secret pathways, ghost roads, trespass zones. We'd walk along ditch-rivers, through fields. The estate we went to live in was still being built but people still took the same shortcut routes – once they walked through potato fields, now they walked through half-built houses, exactly the same journey, but through the new suburbia instead of through the English countryside. The desire paths were still there.

★

We'd go to the Catholic cathedral, where Liverpool becomes Brasilia, on foraging trips, gathering coloured tiles that had fallen off the building's concrete struts, smaller than Scrabble tiles, thin as wafers, pale yellow and blue, our pockets rattling with tiny pieces of sacred architecture. John Piper's stained-glass lantern shining down on us, sunlight shining down on us, like torch beams through sweet wrappers. In the cavities of William Mitchell's fibreglass door sculptures, we'd find spiders weaving webs, the Prophet of Ezekiel's visions of ox, eagle, lion and wild-eyed man, alive with arachnids. I assemble these dreams and visions into my own private cosmos.

Nostalgia is an illness, perhaps. And yet, it's beautiful. I live in memory. I live in the present moment but the past is here too, sometimes shimmering, sometimes dimming in the same space as the now. The blackberries I picked beyond the school fence sixty years ago tasted beautiful and they still taste beautiful now, in the present moment, sixty years after I put them in my mouth. The blue and yellow cathedral tiles are rattling in my pocket in the present moment. I can hear them. Listen! In Ostend, in the hotel bed, nearly fifty years ago, there were tears rolling down my face. I can feel them now. Nostalgia is a fever. It feels like a surrender, a defeat, a negative. I try and resist. I succumb. So be it…

Invisible Maps

Mouth ulcers, ruined mouth, I can hardly speak, can hardly eat. The hotel owner eyes me suspiciously, wondering why I'm soaking the bread roll in milk, ripping off small pieces and placing them on my tongue as if feeding myself the host in some kind of weirdo holy communion. I feel sick. He watches me wanting to be sick, hovering near my table. I put the remaining chunk of bread in my pocket and stand up to leave, shouldering my duffle bag as he produces the bill for the night. It costs the equivalent of £3.00, which makes me think about staying another night and getting myself together, but the owner's already guiding me to the door, taking my Belgian francs, ushering me out into the street. I turn to say thank you, but he's already closed the door. And there I am. I have no sanctuary, it's time to go. In my pocket the chunk of bread and sugar cubes are comforting. I walk in search of a motorway with sugar on my tongue.

Now that Stan has gone – presumably reunited with his cowboy boots in Liverpool – I am alone, frightened, and yet giddy. I've never been so alone, so anonymous, so free. It feels like I am watching myself moving into a new body. The skin I'm in is letting in wild twin.

In the cabin of a truck sitting between the driver's girlfriend and her dog, I imagine invisible maps. Easy hitching, third truck of the morning and we're on our way to Brussels. I can't remember the faces, but I can remember certain gestures, the energy in the vehicle, the movement of cigarettes in hands to lips, the cursive writing of the hands, writing in smoke. The driver's tattooed hands, his girlfriend's bitten fingernails, his smokers cough. It felt as if we were moving forward into a new possibility, rolling down the road into the unexpected space of the next moment. I liked the anxiety, the raw nerve tingle and fear. An interlude before the coming altered state. Forward momentum – the *more forward* you go the less chance there is that you'll turn back. I liked feeling frightened. Fear mixed up with excited chatter and laughter and smoke, the disordered atmosphere of the unknowable. The crammed and noisy cabin of a truck, juddering south to a city I did not know.

The maps I am imagining show boulevards and alleyways, bridges across shadow-rivers, secret hiding places in the ruins. I'm imagining a map of wonders but all I'm seeing is motorways and trucks, petrol stations, car parks. The driver and his girlfriend ask me questions – who am I and where have I come from and where am I going to? I invent myself. I've been travelling for months. I'm a poet. I'm going to Paris to meet my lover. I think they know I'm lying. They laugh, they share their cigarettes and peppermints. And when we get to the northern edge of Brussels, they drop me off and wave goodbye and I'm standing next to an enormous metal crystal, a space station fallen from the sky: Atomium. A science fiction hallucination. I can't decipher its signals. I lie down in the grass and fall asleep.

It rains while I am sleeping, and I wake up cold and wet and my mouth ulcers have ruptured – my whole mouth seems to be falling to pieces and I can hardly speak. In the camera shop, an assistant wants to know why I'm buying a Kodak Instamatic rather than the Olympus he's trying to sell me. He's looking at me closely, wondering why I'm shaking – and coughing now too, a hacking dog cough – wondering why I'm bleeding from the mouth. I mumble something about just needing something to keep a record of things I've never seen before. *Souvenirs.* Ten minutes earlier I stood in the Grand Place, gazing in awe at its beauty. I needed some way of keeping that moment. I can't afford the Instamatic, but I pay for it anyway and go back to the square where I take bad Kodaks of an imaginary city. And while I'm taking a photo of a flower stall, a woman wearing a piece of carpet as a cloak approaches me holding out her hand. She opens up her fingers and holds out to me an offering – a hen's egg. And then she breaks the shell, peels the egg, and offers it to me, miming that I should eat it. A gift of a soft-boiled egg. I take her photograph. This strange, small act of kindness brings tears to my eyes, and as the carpet-wearing woman wanders off, I sit down in a doorway and eat the egg, thinking *this is why I'm here…*

I spend two days in Brussels, mostly getting lost, sleeping in a fleabag hotel, looking into gloomy, tempting bars but worried about money, drinking cough mixture, having nightmares. And then I walk out of the city, heading to Antwerp, which is not on the route to Paris but I'm thinking *what the fuck.* I send a postcard home to my parents saying everything is going well. The photograph on the card is of the Atomium. Not wanting them to know I'm already travelling alone I sign it, *Love from Jeff and Stan.* It takes me eight hours to get to Antwerp. The final driver is so worried about me, he offers to take me to the hospital. When I refuse, he takes me to the youth hostel instead where I reluctantly become a member, thinking *Jack Kerouac wouldn't join the Youth Hostel Association.* I book in and go to bed exhausted. And I think I'm slipping into hallucination, into fever. In a borrowed nylon sleeping bag I lie awake, shaking. The boy in the bunk above me has a pocket transistor radio pressed between his ear and his pillow, tuned into a Russian radio station, muffled voices seep through his mattress into my head. He's fast asleep. I think

I'm absorbing his dreams, demented voyages, looming abyss, Atomium in distorted orbit, constellations of burning cigarettes, sleeping strangers, heavy heaven, Russian voices murmuring. And then in the morning there's no one in the top bunk, no one else in the room.

Pandemic landscapes, diseased skeletons, warzones, mad parades: I wander through the art gallery gazing in wonder and horror at suffering saints and rebel angels. Images becoming part of the fever, the radio transmission. I stand before James Ensor's oil painting *The Intrigue,* masked figures in a wedding portrait, doll baby corpse over a woman's shoulder. (And now I doubt the memory. I went to the gallery, but did I look at the painting? Did I dream it?) It enters my fever. I'm awake but in a dream. And later I sit on a bench on the banks of the river Scheldt, talking to a boy who tells me he is kayaking from the river's source in France to the North Sea. He hopes it takes forever. He says you reach a stage in the journey, all journeys, where you slip over the edge into a different imaginary world, into a molten state of being where anything is possible and you submit, you just pour yourself over the edge into elsewhere. He asks me where I'm going, and I tell him I'm going to Paris. At the same time as I say this, I decide to go to Amsterdam. That night I sleep. In the morning, I pack my bag and head for the road. For Elsewhere.

The man on the hard shoulder on the edge of a town called Boom looks like Kris Kristofferson – long, straggly hair, denim and corduroy, woollen hat pulled down over his ears. He tells me the first lift is his – he's been here for hours, and I have to move further down the slip road so that he's the first hitcher drivers will see. I do as he says, walk as far as is legal, sit on my duffle bag and watch him shuffling, waiting. I've been there ten minutes, and a car comes onto the slip, steams past Kris Kristofferson, slows down a few yards after me, stops. The driver opens the passenger

door and shouts at me to get in. Kristofferson is fuming. I throw
my bag in the car, turn and wave towards him, gesturing to him
to come with me. He throws his bag over his shoulder, runs
down the tarmac, laughing, whooping, and we both jump in the
car. Kristofferson laughs when I tell the driver we go everywhere
together and he replies he's going to Amsterdam, *if that's any use?*
The cigarettes are out – Gitanes – and we're on the move.

Kristofferson, my companion, is on an endless spiritual quest,
has just returned from India, is on his way to Palestine. He smells
of jasmine and he rattles when he moves, with the soft percussion
of his many beads and bracelets. I tell him the truth – I'm a filing
clerk going the wrong way to Paris – and he shows gold teeth as
he laughs with delight. He's the first of several carpenters I will
meet over the next few years. It seems to go with the territory.
He tells me he likes wood, its grain, its tactile nature – but
also because it is impermanent, provisional, it has strength *and*
vulnerability. A table will not last forever but during its lifespan it
serves its worthy purpose. The impermanent and provisional has
value, perhaps more value than the permanent everlasting. Even
wood burning on a bonfire has a reason for being in the world...

We get dropped off in Amsterdam, near the zoo, and we walk
across the city. I can't handle what I'm seeing. Overwhelmed by
the sheer strangeness of the city, of water where you'd expect to
see roads, of bridges over dark canals, of a heron standing next to
a fisherman on Prinsengracht as if teaching his apprentice. A cello
player in an upstairs window plays a concerto, while a man on
the doorstep below has his hair cut by a child, as if Pablo Casals
were living above a salon run by a toddler barber. And trams and
bicycles, bicycles everywhere, and the ringing of their bells.

'Where are you going to stay?' Kristofferson asks me, the stray
dog he's seemingly stuck with. I tell him it hasn't even occurred to

me. I hadn't expected to even be in Amsterdam. I'm supposed to be in Paris. He gives me a look, thinks I'm a complete idiot, takes me to a Christian hostel, the Eben Haezer on Bloemstraat. I pay for three nights and go to sleep on a bunk bed in a dormitory full of healthy-looking travellers, excitedly getting ready for a night on the town. I pull my jacket over my head. I wipe tears from my eyes. I sleep in fever.

Thief of Souls

He rearranges pieces of fabric on his mattress, swatches the size of cigarette packs, scrawled with strange alphabets, hermetic hieroglyphs. He inks his fingertips and presses prints onto the cloths, his signature. He cleans the ink off his fingertips with spit. And then he somehow erases himself from reality, passes through some portal only he can sense, becomes still, transparent. I'm transfixed by his stillness, his emptiness, his open black eyes blind to his surroundings, as if he's looking deep into himself because there's nothing of consequence for him in the world the rest of us inhabit. Hanging around his neck, on a beaded necklace, is a cardboard sign bearing a handwritten statement:

Whosoever Looks at Me Invades
My Body and Steals My Soul

This is the first thing I see when I wake up on my first morning in Amsterdam. Opposite bunk, top bed, draped in robes, and what looks like a prayer mat on his head. This is some kind of demonic presence in a nest of messages and curses. A thief of souls. I'm assuming I'm dead, and this is my guide through purgatory. Up on his bunk he looks as if he's levitating. In silence he arranges his curses, falls into his trance.

★

I buy black pumpernickel bread and a carton of milk in a bakery on Rozengracht and sit on a bench, ripping bread, soaking it in milk, crushing Vitamin C tablets into the gunk, pushing the bread into my mouth, watching the city. I think I'm becoming the protagonist in Knut Hamsun's *Hunger*, which if I'm being honest has always been a subconscious, pathetic ambition. This romantic obsession with the dissolute and wayward inhabitants of my favourite books – this is my downfall. I mean, *look* at me. I am a lost child.

How much weight have I lost? What happened to my hair? This matted, rattail *mess*. I've only been away a few days and I already look like death and need a hospital. I haven't changed my clothes once. The soles of my boots are breaking up. My mouth, my ruined mouth! I traipse to Leidseplein, where I sit and watch a sleight-of-hand magician pulling trinkets from behind the ears of pretty girls. And suddenly the sky is pale blue, my bones are warm for the first time in days. There is music coming from a café and it sounds like a tune that's been composed specifically for this day, for this moment of pale blue, and trinkets conjured from behind the ears. And I breathe and go with unaccustomed joy (is this joy?) into the city (have you ever smelled coffee on the air of an Amsterdam morning?).

> *Dear Mum and Dad,*
> *We're in Amsterdam (slight detour).*
> *You'd love it here!*
> *XX*

Warmoesstraat – a pilgrimage – to the bar where Jean-Baptiste Clamence used to drink. Camus' *The Fall*, an overcoat pocketbook, perhaps the paperback in my pocket in the photograph Hugh took of me in St John's Gardens, wine bottle by my side. Again, as ever, when I first read *The Fall*, I didn't understand it despite its apparent simplicity. I didn't know what I was meant to find beneath, between the words. Again, as ever, this was exactly what I was looking for in a book – its disturbance, its unsettling, strange anxiety.

I'm not prepared for Warmoesstraat. Five years into the future, this street on the edge of the red-light district will be central to my life. On this, my first visit, I feel as if I've walked into the dark dominion of Jacques Brel's *Amsterdam* as sung by David Bowie. I expect to see Jean Genet cruising in an alley. The street has the sordid-damnation-alley-vibe of a degenerate opera. Leather boys in doorways, prostitutes in alleys, a hypodermic needle in the gutter, crushed under my boot, bars full of drinkers, dealers on corners, pickpockets, the *hash, spid, cocaine* whisper of speed walking hustlers, broken neon and ultra-violet flicker. In the centre of all this stands the police station, cops leaning on patrol cars outside, smoking and laughing, yards away from dealers. The atmosphere of the street is damp, oppressive, heavy, maritime. Even the light is heavy. On Zeedijk's bridges, heroin dealers hustle in clouds of spliff-smoke. It's an ugly, frightening hellhole, and I feel like I've arrived.

I don't buy cannabis. I don't buy heroin. I don't go down an alleyway for a fifteen minute 'appointment' with a prostitute. I go into a snack bar and buy a carton of orange juice and a Snickers, and I stand on the corner of Warmoesstraat and Lange Niezel and watch the mad parade. Here we are in the *cold, wet place where a thick blanket of fog constantly hangs over the crowded, neon-light-lined streets.* This is Albert Camus, who also asks: *Have you noticed that Amsterdam's concentric canals resemble the circles of hell? The middle-class hell, of course, peopled with bad dreams. When one comes from the outside, as one gradually goes through those circles, life – and hence its crimes – becomes denser, darker. Here, we are in the last circle.*

★

It's there, all around me – it's there right now, pouring into this room in Liverpool. The bad dreams, the denser, darker atmosphere of the street. I can even smell the mayonnaise stench coming from the automat and a hint of amylnitrate.

At the Zeedijk end of the street I stop outside Warmoesstraat 91, once the Mexico City bar where Jean-Baptiste tells his story to the stranger. When Camus passed through Amsterdam sometime in the 1950s, did he drink in Mexico City? Did he meet a drinker at the bar who then told him his tale? Is the book a transcribed tape recording of an actual confession? Well, that's the way I read it. Book as document, real event. The bar in the book is long gone, it's now an exhausted looking café. I look inside for Albert and Jean-Baptiste, ghosts. But there are only backpackers from the Kabul Hostel, reading their *Let's Go Europe* books and supping the foam off their beers. Joseph Roth was here in 1936, holed up in the Hotel Eden writing *Confessions of a Murderer*, drinking himself into a stupor in the brown cafés, drowning in Bols Genever and scribbling in notebooks. Warmoesstraat *feels* like a Roth street, a nightmare alley you voluntarily succumb to despite your angels telling you to leave.

I walk down Lange Niezel into the heart of the Red-Light district. A glass of beer in the Old Sailors bar, watching the crowd, the women in windows glowing in UV light. A gutter-perfume in the air of mayonnaise, detergent and lubricant. It's like Wardour Street distorted, off its face on shit lager and poppers, a mash up of sleaze-nightmare and pretty postcard picturesque. Delft pottery souvenirs next door to dildos. Striptease joint door hustlers calling out their *Real Live Fucky-Fucky* spiel, pounding disco music, old women walking dogs, Hells Angels wearing Oakland chapter colours, businessmen window shopping for a lunchtime shag, a smoking priest.

I'm looking for signs of revolution. Somewhere in these streets and warehouses, in the 1960s, the countercultural revolutionary Provos group constructed effigies to burn. Schooled on anarchist pamphlets purchased in Liverpool's News from Nowhere bookshop, I'm drawn to the idea of ritual interventions in the urban everyday. Exorcisms. Dada art pranks. Surrealist provocations, disrupting the bourgeois surface. Underground subversives, the Provos had the charisma of outlaw intellectuals, artists ripping up the fabric of convention. At the Little Darling sculpture on Spui, the artist and 'Prophet of Magic Amsterdam', Robert Jasper Grootveld danced his midnight rituals in clouds of smoke. Perhaps if you listen you can hear his incantation, *Uche, uche, uche! Klaas komt! Klaas is coming!* His voice echoing off the surrounding buildings, calling for revolt, waking addicted consumers from their slumber. The Provo symbol of rebellion, *ANTI* – scrawled on walls. Dutch teddy boys – the Nozems – mutating into actionists and underground magicians of dissent. I go to look at *krakhuisen,* the squatted warehouses where, unknown to me at this time, I will later spend my days. Memories of my future self, walking through lucid dreams.

Down at the Westerdok, I walk past squats and abandoned warehouses and the black murk and oil rainbow waters of the dock. In the shell of a wooden hut, I find a scrawny apple tree, pale green fruit hanging like pagan tree decorations. Winter apples. I pick one, bite into it, mouth filling with juice as sour as lemon, stinging my mouth ulcers, sharp as needles. I feel a very long way from home, and I can't remember why I ever left it. But this is good, this place, these collapsing ruins and the cormorants drying their wings on the broken wharf. I pick another apple and put it in my jacket pocket. It somehow keeps me going, like a battery. I keep hold of it, starlight in my hand.

★

Time travel, following myself through the streets of Amsterdam nearly fifty years ago. This is the city, the hallucination. Melancholy angels in a secret church and a derelict gasworks sinking into the mud; cormorants like tattered Christs on the rotting hulk of a tugboat; I fall in love with a magical illusion – Tuschinski's Art Deco cinema like a cathedral made from meteorites and rocket ships; in a side street, a cigar-maker in his workshop doorway, skin the colour of his papery tobacco leaves; a naked pensioner on his flat-tired bicycle winding his way through the Dam Square crowds; Duke Ellington's *Prelude to a Kiss* coming out of a jazz dive on Marnixstraat like the ghost of Johnny Hodges; clock-headed men in Ed Kienholz's *Beanery*, ten-past-ten smiles on their faces.

I sit in Vondelpark with Kristofferson. He passes me his spliff. The dog ends of the counterculture are all around us. Straggle-haired hippies lying on the slopes in their makeshift bivouacs. A geriatric cosmonaut, off his head on chemicals, washing his armpits in scoops of water from the lake. Jugglers, too, and Kristofferson shaking his head in dismay. We sit there wondering how the revolution turned into a circus act. This is the place where Amsterdam became an outpost of Haight-Ashbury. The playful rebellion of Love Ins, Be Ins, Happenings, psychedelic dream rituals, *provocatie*, Dadaist interventions, Speaker's Corner debates about the atomic bomb and Vietnam. The revolutionary utopia is now embodied in a woman in tie-die trying to interest us in her basket of homemade hash cakes. Kristofferson has been everywhere, and up until this trip I've only ever been on holidays with the family. Caravan sites in Prestatyn and B&Bs in Woolacombe aren't quite the same as Palestine and Marrakesh. He builds another spliff and says we missed the revolution. He gives me ten loose pages torn out of his *Let's Go Europe*, some vitamin C, a pair of gloves and a sewing kit. I tell him I'm thinking of going to Hamburg and he gives me a fatherly advice face. He tells me I need to look after myself, that I'll come unstuck and run out of money if I keep going in the wrong direction. The ten loose pages are all about Paris. He tells me to go to Paris and do what I set out to do.

I spot the hieroglyph man from the hostel, shuffling down Broewersgracht, a shawl covering his head. I follow him. He scuttles down Willemsstraat, pauses to look in the window of a shop that sells nothing but antique spectacles, disappears into the gloom of a café in the shadow of the Noorderkirk. I follow him inside, but he's gone, just the dust of his shadow, the malevolent shade. And when I get back to the Eben Haezer he's in his position, his placard hanging around his neck, his messages and warnings scattered around his bedsheet. His presence is unbearable, malignant. No one else seems concerned, which focuses the intensity of his presence on me. I feel like I'm being dragged into the orbit of a death-star in human form. I take my wild apple out of my pocket and place it on my bed. He stares at it for a moment and then he covers his eyes with his blindfold, as if the intensity is too much for him, apple starlight shining in his eyes.

Nighttime. The insomniacs are out, and their dreams are in the sky. I missed the hostel curfew so I'm walking the canals in the rain, ugly weather, night-clouds above, and down here on the market square there's a man howling like a dog at another man who appears to be dancing, staggering, offering his damp cigarette to the gods. I stand on the cobbles, watching a ballet, the ragged beauty of his dance. He turns, sees me standing there, asks me a question: *Have you fallen far?* I laugh, point at the sky and tell him, *Yes, I fell from there.* He nods – seems reasonable. He shrugs and goes back to his ballet, the damp cigarette his guiding light.

In the morning I pack my bag and deliberately bid a pleasant goodbye to the thief of souls. He stares at me with a look of admonishment, points at his placard as if to remind me of the regulations. Kristofferson is asleep in his bunk. I slip out before he wakes and walk to the train station, conscious that I'll never see him again, wondering how I'll cope without my guardian angel. Amsterdam on a Sunday morning looks as bleak as any other city – graffiti-shuttered shops, Saturday night litter, Kalverstraat looking grim in the early morning light. Looking back, I should have stayed, looked for a job in the tulip fields, a hotel job. Amsterdam had everything I wanted – the beauty of the canal streets, the sleaze of Oudezijds, Congolese weed, the street markets and cafés. I wanted to stay. I didn't want to stay. I wanted to keep moving, something reckless kept driving me to the edge. It wasn't as if I didn't see the danger – most of the time I was frightened and imagined danger all around me. Paris, I had to get to Paris.

At the train station I buy a one-way ticket to Brussels. I've had it with hitching, for now. On the train I eat the apple.

Eat the apple, eat the fear.

Ghost Theatre

My dad would give me books. From childhood onwards, up until just a few years ago, he'd turn up with a holdall like a door-to-door librarian. He didn't read any of these books, but he somehow knew I'd love them. He would watch me taking them out of the holdall, enjoying my curiosity. Beatrix Potter when I was a child or Spike Milligan's *Silly Verse for Kids*. An illustrated *Steadfast Tin Soldier*, which filled my dreams with voyages down gutters and into the mouths of fish. They could be anything, random finds in auction rooms – Thomas Browne's *Urn Burial*, *Funk and Wagnall's Dictionary*, Ruskin's *Unto This Last*, *The Anathemata* by David Jones. Denton Welch's *Journals* became a lifelong obsession. I've still got the miniature, complete works of Shakespeare in a small leather-bound box, an antique travellers' library. Later, there were surprising contemporary novels such as Don Delillo's *White Noise* and the strangest one of all – William T. Vollman's *You Bright and Risen Angels,* which he'd bought in a job lot of first editions in an auction room in Hoylake. *How was the book, what was it about?* he'd ask, and I suppose on that occasion I must have replied that it was kind of about an insect war against the inventors of electricity.

My lack of ambition, my aversion to work, obviously made having a steady job acutely embarrassing. It interfered with cinema matinees, afternoons in boozers, and digging for holy-grail records and books in Probe and Atticus. It interfered with

Howie Chaykin, Angela Carter, cosmic funk, Krazy Kat, Crème de Menthe and Southern Comfort, Josie and the Pussycats, Anna Kavan, Army & Navy Stores surplus clothing, Richard Brautigan, Higsons Bitter, Pauline Boty, Patrick McGoohan, Dagmar Krause, Laurence Harvey, Old Peculiar, Niki de Sainte Phalle, Dirk Bogarde on daytime TV, Theodore Sturgeon, Lebanese Red, The Partridge Family, Captain Scarlet, Heathcote Williams, Betty Boop, Enrico Cadillac Junior, Edie Sedgwick and Candy Darling, Ron Mael's moustache, Anthony Burgess, kung fu films, Smallcreep's Day, Delmore Schwarz, R. D. Laing and Nico. And smoking weed in the key park.

Sometimes on Friday nights my dad and I would go to the Liverpool Stadium to watch the all-in wrestling. I loved the antics of the old women in the audience, their geriatric burlesque show of violence and obscenity. I loved it just as much as the antics of the leotard-clad showmen in the ring. To me, the grapplers were just like pop stars, cabaret singers settling the odds. Adrian Street with his glam rock Diva pout and flounce, like Bowie's Queen Bitch, *swishy in his satin and tat;* Kendo Nagasaki leaning on his van in the carpark, a samurai warrior from Shropshire with a touch of getaway-driver heft. We'd sup hot Bovril in a plastic cup, laughing at the vaudeville, me and my dad.

Ghost archive, slide projections in the skull, watching memories on the bedsheet pinned up on the parlour wall. Memory of moving into the new house, the garden an overgrown rubble dump, weeds as tall as I was, a single red tulip blazing up against the garage wall. Mrs Blundell, my infant school teacher at Gwladys Street drove us there in her bright red Mini, dropped us off with mop and bucket, waved goodbye and drove away. Mum, Val, baby Kathryn and I stand in the new house, mum's dream house where her dreams will grow. Dad at work in the print factory, mum going into the garden wasteland, pulling half-bricks out of the dirt. No birds, no life, oak tree shadow turning the garden grey. At the far end there's a ditch and a wire fence looking out onto a farm field and building site. Other houses just like this one are being built and the town is going to grow and grow, and fields will disappear. When dad comes home, we all start to dig. Liverpool is a world away; I wonder if we'll ever go back there. I don't quite understand this new, strange place we've moved to. When I ask my dad how long we'll be here he answers, *Four or five years.* Fifty years have passed and he's still there.

When I was eight and I realised Liverpool still existed and it was possible to go there, it came as a relief. It was somewhere we would *go to* rather than *live in,* it was a place we'd drive to, now that we had a car. We'd go and visit the grandparents, the uncles, the people who kept us connected to the city. Every night my grandparents would read The Deaths in *The Echo,* 'I see Edith Milburn has passed, *peacefully at home.'* And then the silence, the prayer hollowing of the atmosphere as we sat sending our thoughts to the dead woman, to her loved ones. I didn't understand this ritual, but I loved it. I loved the silent space and the fact that grandma in particular seemed to know a new dead person every single day. There then comes a point when uncles who own butchers' shops stop being butchers and go to work in car factories or on the market where they sell anything they can. Uncle Ron sells past-its-sell-by-date tinned food from the city council's secret nuclear fallout shelter, rumoured to be somewhere underneath the city library. We don't know how Uncle Ron came to have the tins in his possession – we don't ask but we do enjoy the beans. The aunties smoke, watch cowboy films, talk about their ailments. The grandparents have always been old, but they were younger than I am now.

When I'd go to auction sales with my dad, he'd buy job-lots of household goods cleared from dead people's houses. We would bring it all back to the new house and store it in the garage: it was a way of bringing pieces of Liverpool back home with us and saving the memories trapped inside the objects. Dad would spend hours in the garage sorting through the relics of these ghosts; my sister Val and I saw the garage as our secret theatre. In its crowded shadows we became a theatre company, acting out the fairytales we loved. Rumpelstiltskin – Val working the old mangle like a spinning wheel, me playing the imp, sewing gold in exchange for her jewellery. Or we'd act out *The Steadfast Tin Soldier* – I'd be swallowed up into a bedside cupboard which doubled as the belly of a fish. We made aeroplanes out of stepladders and a dustbin. We made tents out of yards of fabric my dad brought home from Indian wholesalers in town, hiding places, nests.

There are certain places in the city – even now – where the trace elements of ancestors are watching. My great grandfather Mick – the illiterate street waif who spent years in the workhouse for consorting with undesirables – is still there now, on West Derby Road, walking to the cobbler's shop he worked in all his life after leaving the workhouse with a shoe mender's skills. He's there now, in my dad's pale blue eyes, the blue eyes I couldn't look into on the morning I left to hitch to Paris. The ancestors are here.

On the train to Brussels, I am thinking about my dad and the room in that house. I am thinking of the things that neither of us could say, the words we didn't even know were there to be said so instead we chose silence. In this contemplation of silence, homesickness is growing.

Permafrost

No one knows where I am and that's the way I like it. I am lost. I've even lost my map so could be anywhere on this cold morning in March, standing at the side of a road, somewhere in Belgium. God knows where.

I went to the tourist information office in Brussels, got a free map, worked out a route and started walking. I walked all day through the city, through places that looked just like the slum areas of Liverpool, through suburbs, through a stretch of tenements where a fat man in a rope-tied raincoat followed me, trousers unzipped, scratching his dirty underpants. I walked wearily until I reached a motorway on the southern edge of the city, where I hitched five lifts to somewhere else, to this roadside in the early morning light.

Away from the road, in a hollow, a circle of caravans, trucks and trailers are parked up next to a ditch. Travellers. A woman is cooking something in a pot over an oil drum fire. Maybe if I go over there, they'll offer me coffee, bread. I'll warm myself at the fire. I don't go, I'm too scared. Then two young boys playing in the camp start walking towards me, curious about the idiot standing in the sleet. Urchin kids, grown-up boots, grease-monkey boiler suits. One of the boys kicks a can towards me, I kick it back. They laugh. We kick the can around for a while, until I kick it into the road and it gets crushed by a truck. We laugh, I shrug an apology. They want to know what I'm doing there – I think that's what they want to know, I can't speak French, I can't speak any languages, I don't think they're speaking French anyway. Romanian, perhaps. I sit down on my bag, and they squat down nearby. One of them says, 'Cigarette?' I laugh, he shrugs, takes out a bent cigarette and lights it with a match. He's about eight years old. They pass the cigarette back and forth, deep smoking expertly. Then one of them goes into the road, dodging cars, retrieves the crushed can and hands it to me. 'Souvenir!' They walk away, laughing, back to the camp. I hold my souvenir.

According to Arthur Rimbaud, the poet becomes a seer by means of a long, immense and systematic derangement of all the senses. Perhaps I thought this journey was an apprenticeship and I would write Beat poetry about wild freedom and the wonders of the road. In truth, I hardly ever felt freedom or lightness, escape or flight: I felt weight, stasis, surge and drag, fear. I'd wake up thinking I was still asleep. I'd sleep, dreaming I was still awake. And this is the point where I realise I don't know why I'm doing this. It's not as if I'm running away from anything. I'm a fugitive with no reason to run away. A fugitive from myself. I am existing in some nowhere place of movement, all directionless lurch and hesitation in places – and in between places – that aren't Liverpool, aren't home. When I was dreaming of being elsewhere, when I longed to be in other places, it made sense to me to rewild myself in strange territories and unfamiliar surroundings. Now that I am inside these territories, I am bewildered, genuinely lost.

Maybe I have already achieved what I set out to do – I've disappeared – and it's a completely futile experience of despair and dread. And I start laughing. Laughing at my own stupidity and carelessness. I go into a general store across the road and look for something to eat. I'm terrified of running out of money so all I buy is a bag of salted peanuts. The woman behind the counter looks at me with pity, asks me if I'm a tourist, which makes me laugh. I go back to my hitching spot and eat the peanuts. A mangy dog from the travellers' camp checks me out, sniffing at my boots. The dog is me, my mongrel spirit animal. I talk to him; he starts to howl.

The temperature drops, the sleet becomes snow. There is ice on the gravel and passing cars splash me with shards and dirty water from clogged gutters and oil puddles. I can feel the cold eating into my bones, and I begin to think, *this is fucking it then... this is where I die...* The temperature is falling. The ground is getting harder. I want to lie down to rest my body, but I'm scared the cold will kill me. The sky is the colour of warships and as cold as the ground. The sky is falling down. I am becoming part of the frozen earth. I am permafrost. The people in the cars have come to see the permafrost. They slow down to look at me, staring in dismay at how easily a man can become frozen, geological material.

Rain, snow and hail, those are the Lower Orders, writes Werner Herzog in *Of Walking in Ice.*

I pull every item of clothing out of my bag and put on my spare jumper, two T-shirts, two spare shirts, and then I put my spare jeans on over the jeans I'm already wearing, ending up looking like I've put on a stone in weight. I jump up and down, thumb out, hitching and dancing. And – understandably – absolutely no one stops to offer me a lift, and so I start to walk. My duffle bag is almost empty. I wear it like a cloak, like a Medieval revenant, staggering through rain and sleet.

Books did this to me. If someone stopped and asked me why I'm lost in the middle of Belgium and potentially dying from hypothermia in the middle of a field, my honest – and ridiculous – answer would be, *Flights of great lyrical beauty in a Picador paperback.* I am being killed by Louis Aragon. It all makes perfect sense. *Paris Peasant* is my death warrant. All the tattered books, the fever-books, the combustible materials. I bought *Paris*

Peasant – we all bought *Paris Peasant* – because it was a Picador, spinning on the bookstore carousel with Beckett and Calvino, with *Smallcreep's Day* and Fritz Zorn's *Mars*. Having bought every Richard Brautigan and Angela Carter, it was time to buy this strange book with the boater-wearing dandy on the cover sitting outside the Liqueurs Bar, beneath a naked beauty gazing down from an upstairs window, single rose in hand. *'Once again, the light splits as it traverses imagination's prism, and I submit to this iridescent universe. What did you think you were up to, my friend, out there on the frontiers of reality?'* What a book for a highly impressionable teenager to read! You base your actions and decisions on sentences in paperbacks. You're dressed like this because Jack Kerouac told you to in *Dharma Bums* – flannel lumberjack shirts, canvas jacket and mountain boots and jeans. You're hitching because of Kerouac, because of these words and you're heading/not heading to Paris and hitching in the wrong direction: *April in Paris, sleet in Pigalle, and last moments. – In my skidrow hotel it was cold and still sleeting so I put on my old blue jeans, old muffcap, railroad gloves and zip-up rain jacket, the same clothes I'd worn as a brakeman in the mountains of California and as a forester in the Northwest, and hurried across the Seine to Les Halles for a last supper of fresh bread and onion soup and pate...* Some kind of degraded ideal of boho, Beat, dissolute-bum writer identity. An adolescent, unarticulated urge to become the lowlife outsider hoodlum poet... and where that gets you is here. A desolate field of mud.

I get to a point where I can't walk any further. The ground is now solid ice, and my boots won't grip. It's all gone a bit Werner Herzog. As often happens when things go shit-shaped I start to laugh, hysterically, staggering to a halt on permafrost, sitting down on the wall of a ditch-bridge, staring into the junk-strewn gully below. Pop cans, bollards, hubcaps, gas cylinders. The romance of travel. I rummage in my duffle bag for something to eat but all I can find is *The Mote in God's Eye,* the bloody Larry Niven book, which is damp now and broken down the spine. A truck bearing GB stickers drives past, completely ignoring me when I run after it shouting, *I'm from England! Please, please...* And then as I spin around, I notice a motorway running parallel to the road I'm on, so I climb over a fence into a farm field where it's easier to walk in mud than it is to walk on ice. I start walking, following the traffic, walking through fields, climbing through hedges and over walls. And when I'm in the depths of my despair and about to lie down defeated on the ground, I notice a flatbed truck slowing down, the driver waving at me, calling out in French, gesturing me to go to him. He pulls over on the hard shoulder, looks and laughs at the state of me – at this bedraggled mess. I climb in. He drives, his painting and decorating gear rattling on the flatbed, the smell of turpentine filling up the cab. We drive for hours, and I have no idea where we're going until we reach a town called Malmedy, where he takes me into a house and presents me to his mother, presumably explaining to her how he found me, miles from nowhere, striding through fields, evidently deranged. She sits me down at the kitchen table and places a bowl of haricot bean soup before me with a chunk of bread and a wedge of cheese. *Eat,* she says, *Eat.*

When I worked at the council I used to sit at my desk and look at maps. Maps of the city, maps of the Mersey from source to sea, maps of other lands. And when I was a child, I loved to look at hand drawn adventure maps in story books. *Treasure Island, A Wizard of Earthsea, Winnie the Pooh.* The maps were as interesting as the story. I used to draw my own maps to accompany books I was reading, and I'd draw maps of treasure islands with an X to mark the spot. According to the folding map of Europe I'd brought with me, there was no such place as Malmedy. I must have invented it in my mad, staggering journey across the permafrost. And if I'd invented Malmedy, it followed that I'd invented the driver of the flatbed truck and his mother and the bowl of haricot bean soup, and the bed I was now lying on in the attic room of the house. I'd gone from hell to heaven in the space of a few hours, and all because I'd seemingly invented a town in Belgium. Sleep is broken, dreams are broken, the journey is broken, the body is broken, the camera is broken, the sky is broken, everything is broken, the bloody stupid *Mote in God's Eye* book is broken.

I wake at noon the following day and, feeling a momentary calmness, creep downstairs to the kitchen, not sure of the rules, the protocols of being an accidental guest. A freeloader, perhaps? A bum… isn't this who the feckless hitchhiker is? Malmedy exists, I can see it through the window, and I can see the painter and decorator loading up his truck. I go outside and ask him how far it is to Paris. It's 240 miles. How long will it take me to get there? He assumes I'm walking, shrugs, laughs, 'At least twelve days.' He tells me I was talking in my sleep and then he tells me I was sleepwalking and then he tells me I was crying, and I had a fever, so they guided me back to bed and calmed me down and left me there to rest. He doesn't seem to mind. He acts as if it's normal to take a complete stranger into your home and feed him bean soup and let him sleep in the attic. Perhaps this *is* normal in Malmedy. Perhaps this is the way things should be, the taking-in of accidental guests, kindness to complete strangers. On the kitchen table, dried on the fire shelf and sellotaped together, rests *The Mote in God's Eye*.

We're taking a spin around Malmedy racetrack in the painter and decorator's renovated 1950s Austin Healey, hurtling around the bends, speeding down the blacktop. He's talking as we go, telling me all about the near fatal accident he had a year ago, upside down and dragged along the track. I'm losing confidence in his custodianship of my mental and physical health. I'm losing my grip on sanity. I close my eyes. Migraine fractals zigzag and rotate across the inside of my eyelids, auras of geometry at once beautiful and disturbing. I focus on the cinematic beauty of the shapes as we hurtle around in circles, a psychedelic lightshow projected on the inside of my skull. And when we stop, he turns to me and remarks how good it is to see me, so relaxed as if in meditation. *Most people are frightened, but you look almost serene.*

Back at the house, I sit at the kitchen table watching his mum baking bread. There's an enormous fruit bowl on the table, full of apples and she puts one on a plate, nodding at me to eat it. She wraps two more apples and two bread rolls in a napkin. I sense it's time to go. Her son comes in and we sit drinking coffee, the three of us, temporary friends. And then when it's time to leave his mother stands on the steps, waving a tea towel in the air, a slow-motion farewell, like a moment in a film. The painter and decorator drops me at the edge of town on a country lane heading vaguely south. He hugs me goodbye. *Bon chance.* And then I'm on my own again, walking down the lane, into 240 miles of highway, into migraine aura sky.

In the madness, I have the ridiculous idea of going in search of Arthur Rimbaud. He's got to be around here somewhere. I veer off course, climb a gate and follow the weather. Charleville must be around here, if only I could get beyond these endless, fucking fields. Years later I did the maths and realised I was at least a hundred miles away but at the time it seemed to be a logical development, a pilgrimage. I'd come to Rimbaud via Bob Dylan and Patti Smith, the poet I'd fallen headlong for after seeing a photograph of her in the NME. *Piss Factory* was, still is, a wake-up call, a call to arms. *And I will travel light, Oh, watch me now.* The streetwise swagger of Patti's delivery, as if through a mouth full of chewing gum and spit, this pissed off rant against convention was like a manifesto for unruly disobedience. Years later, hearing her recite it at a gig in Manchester as Lenny Kaye sent squalls of noise into the darkness, made me cry. The barely coherent rage and sass of the story, like a made-on-the-cheap arthouse movie about a fucked up runaway with attitude: *I figured I was speedo motorcycle... And I'm gonna go, I'm gonna get out of here... Never return, never return, to burn out in this piss factory, And I will travel light. Oh, watch me now.*

In my friend Mark Blanchard's bedroom in those mid-70s years, we would read the music papers and listen to the radio, recording songs on cheap cassettes, songs that were somehow passing on secret information – Television's *Little Johnny Jewel*, almost beyond our understanding but at the same time seeming as if it were beamed directly into this bedroom in the dark, especially for us. And the first time we heard *Marquee Moon* on John Peel, guitars like coded signals, the bedroom filling up with Verlaine and Lloyd's quicksilver ghosts: *I remember, Ooh, how the darkness doubled, I recall, Lightning struck itself, I was listening, Listening to the rain, I was hearing, Hearing something else...* On the radio, Pere Ubu sending messages from devastated industrial zones: *At night I can see the stars on fire, I can see the world in flames, It's all because of you, or your thousand other names...* Songs like samizdat bulletins, sonic grenades. I'd rip photographs of rock stars and poets out of magazines and Sellotape them into scrapbooks. Somewhere I still have a collage I made of Rimbaud, Patti Smith, Lou Reed, Lenny Bruce and Billy the Kid, a firmament of outlaws. Mark is *becoming* Patti Smith. Typing up poems and lyrics, growing his hair, soon he'll be wearing eye shadow and painting his fingernails black, singing songs into his cassette recorder. Cassettes are captured dreams. When Mark moves to London to put a band together, I sometimes hitch down and stay in his Kings Cross squat, sleeping on a mattress in his kitchen. He writes a song called *Days of Wine and Roses* about his father and it makes me cry. In Atticus Books, because Patti Smith told me to, I bought *Illuminations* in the New Directions edition, purely because I fell in love with Rimbaud's face in Ray Johnson's image on the cover, punk before punk had even been invented. *I am the walker on the great highway… I gaze for a long time at the melancholy gold laundry of the setting sun.* Because Lou Reed told me to, I buy Delmore Schwartz's *In Dreams Begin Responsibilities* and try and write short stories on my insect typewriter.

So, all of this is going on in my head as I stride across the fields, and I am not even remotely heading in the direction of Arthur Rimbaud's birthplace. I climb into a derelict truck and sit there in the driving seat, nodding off, exhausted, fingers stained with rust. *Filing Clerk Found Dead in Rusted Truck in Belgian Field.* It's either a newspaper headline or the title of a book of poems. The only lift I can get is in the wreckage from a road accident. I walk again, even though I want to submit to the oozing earth, and after a few hours of this I reach a road where there's a sign pointing the way to Luxembourg. With some relief, I decide that's where I'm going.

And that's why, somewhere in the north of Luxembourg, in a scraggy wood near the border, I wake up. Luxembourg wasn't on my itinerary, but it was the best that I could manage, and once I'd crossed the border, I'd decided to have a nap but must have slept for hours. Cold and wet but still alive. I know I'm still alive because I'm being prodded with a walking stick by a boy who thinks I'm dead. He asks me what I'm doing. I think he's speaking Dutch. I tell him I'm just catching up on sleep and he sits down next to me, offers me half a sandwich. We eat his ham sandwich even though I don't eat meat. He tells me he's from Groeningen and he likes to spend his weekends hitching as far as he can on the Saturday and hitching back to Groeningen on Sunday. Strapped to his enormous rucksack there's an entire kitchen – camping stove, saucepan, tin mug, spatula, even a wok. He wears thick bottle-bottom glasses held together with parcel tape, and his hair looks like an old lady's perm gone badly wrong in the wash. His name is something like Grokl, like a phlegmy clearing of the throat. We drink his coffee and then we head for the blacktop. Even though Grokl looks awful on the road, he's a genius at hitchhiking and we get to Luxembourg in two fast rides. Then we hitch to Echternach where he knows a good hostel, and he doesn't think I can afford to stay in Luxembourg so I should go with him. Of course, Echternach is in the east and I'm supposed to be heading west. To Paris.

As soon as we get to Echternach I decide to head back to Luxembourg, say goodbye to a disappointed Grokl, get stuck on the road next to the Radio Luxembourg transmission masts and wait for hours for a lift which takes me *back* to Echternach. The driver, Peter, looks like Gunter Grass and throughout the journey he feeds me with a constant supply of throat lozenges and Parma Violets. He has the large but gentle demeanour of a St Bernard dog. I feel rescued. We go for a beer in a bar in the middle of nowhere and I'm ashamed to say I hold my penknife in my fist, just in case he attacks me. I don't know why I was so wary of this gentle soul. He has watery eyes and speaks softly through his moustache, enjoying watching me sip my beer. And when we drive into town, he drops me off at the hostel and invites me for supper later. In the hostel garden, Grokl is set up in his portable kitchen, flamboyantly cooking ratatouille for anyone who's hungry and soundtracking his cooking performance with Emerson, Lake and Palmer on a portable cassette player. He reminds me of Mrs McVeigh, that Domestic Science teacher who set her blue rinse hair on fire. A party of schoolboys crowd around me asking if my mother knows where I am, and will she be worried about me travelling alone so far from home. I think about the postcards home, the lie that Stan is still with me. I feel homesick. I eat Grokl's ratatouille and try and ignore Keith Emerson's hideous organ racket. None of this is exactly *On the Road*, none of this is exactly Jack Kerouac. But it will have to do…

★

In the evening I go to Peter's cottage for supper, and he fills me up on bread and cheese, slices of ham (which I fold up and hide in my jacket pocket), pickles and gherkins and glasses of cloudy beer. The house is like your auntie's, antimacassars on the chairbacks, embroidered place mats on the Ercol dining table. We hardly speak, awkwardly moving around the cottage, which he seems to be too big for. We sit watching television. He fiddles with the aerial and manages to find *Coronation Street*. We watch Elsie Tanner and Ena Sharples, the pair of us sitting side by side in armchairs like a married couple happy with their lives. It gets late and I have to get back to the hostel before curfew. We hug and say goodbye. Peter stands at his gate, hand in air, calling *Goodnight Godfrey* until I reach the end of the lane.

Lucid Dreamer

Nighttime in a Citroen 2cv for 100 miles, driving through rain with a businessman who's quite understandably irritable with me because my French is next to non-existent. I completely agree with him. It's pathetic. Poor man, long journey in the dark, hoping for some company and smalltalk about French football or television and he gets me, an *English idiot.* I tell him about the day I just spent in Luxembourg after hitching in from Echternach. He asks me where I ate and I tell him I ate sitting on a bench in the park, eating bread and oranges, that I stole from a supermarket. And a strawberry waffle that an old lady gave me because she thought I was homeless. He is appalled. I despise myself as much as he does and we spend most of the journey in sullen silence – nearly three hours of awkward, empty, Citroen-sized claustrophobia and shrug, a sense of dreams unfulfilled – both mine and his – filling the car like fumes… but what were the dreams anyway?

I had dreamed of altered states, the tilting of the axis and the changing of the writing on the wall. The day of the ladybirds, when everything was possible, when Liverpool became a beautiful, demented hybrid of architecture and insect. I remember that day so clearly – even now, today, fifty years later, gazing in awe at the churning red ocean of bugs carpeting the pavements and walls of Old Hall Street, that Cronenberg day I walked to work, ankle deep in the insect plague. The sight of shorthand typists, clerical officers, bank clerks scooping up handfuls of writhing bugs, tiptoeing over carcasses, the sound of laughter, the sense of awe, of being an actor in a mad, avantgarde opera. I can pinpoint that day as the dawning of the great realisation that everything, anything was possible. If a science fiction event on this scale was possible, surely it must be possible to alter the course of your own life? I remember going home after work and telling my parents about it. They had no idea it had even happened, but here and there, in the garden and on the windows, there were stray ladybirds, windblown away from the plague mass in the city. Perhaps sometimes it takes a plague of ladybirds to wake you from your dream, into a more lucid dream of possibility.

I tried to talk to my dad about change, about what I didn't want to be. He'd be working in the garage on some broken piece of furniture, filling in wormholes, staining a veneer. We never said much – I'd just pass him things he needed – or he'd show me a pile of music hall 78s, or tell me with delight about that landscape print that turned out to be a watercolour. His hands were sepia brown and black, coloured with wood stain and printers' ink – the brown from the furniture, the black from the printing factory where he still worked shifts. His dreams were in this garage and in the auction rooms and junk shops of the city. One day he would get out of the factory and realise his dream of being a secondhand furniture man. He knew what he wanted to be but did the thing he had to. It was just what it was, the way things had to be when you have a family and a mortgage and responsibilities. *You can't just go off on your adventures forever. That's not the way life works.* Sometimes we'd talk about music. He didn't think Slade's *Skweeze Me, Pleeze Me* was a patch on *Gudbuy T'Jane* and, as ever, wanted to know why Marc Bolan wore girls' shoes. Bryan Ferry was too old to be going out dressed like that and *Motown Chartbusters Volume 7* was not the best in the series by any stretch. Sneaking into a New Year's Eve party in the house next door, my sister Val and I were mortified to witness my mum and dad and several neighbours striding around in a circle, punching the air with *one gloved hand* and stamping their feet to T. Rex's *Children of the Revolution*. When I asked him about it the following day he replied, *Why not? It's a really good song.* My parents seemed far too old to be behaving like this, but I realise now they were only in their forties. In retrospect, this moment of joyous abandon is beautiful, but at the time I wanted the ground to open up and swallow me. How happy they were, Mum and Dad. How happy they always seemed to be. The printing factory wasn't where my dad wanted to be, but he had all this, this family, this neighbourhood. He had his garage full of furniture to lovingly restore. He had dancing to pop music at parties. He had love.

There was a Rosedale Electric Chord Organ in the garage – the type of organ David Bowie used on *Memory of a Free Festival* on the *Space Oddity* LP. My sister Kathryn and I used to compose songs, rehearsing one song in particular that sounded like The Residents if they'd formed a band in kindergarten. *I don't think I want to stay here, I must be upon my way here, say 'goodbye' and 'cheerio' dear, time to say goodbye...*

Outside Reims Cathedral I say goodbye to the Citroen driver. He shrugs – the shrug of disdain – and drives away, and once again I'm alone and the rain is now a storm. I have dreams about cathedrals, I've had them all my life. I dream of cathedrals inside cathedrals, an infinity of Matryoshka cathedrals and the gargoyles and gurning monks carved into their stone. I stand there in the rain and I'm standing looking at my dream.

There are two men huddled in the cathedral doorway, passing a bottle back and forth like down-and-out priests. The rain's heavier now so I stand on the edge of the cathedral entrance, not sure if I'm allowed inside the men's shelter, nodding to them, hesitating. They give each other a bemused glance and then shuffle to one side to

make room for me. The three of us stand there, watching the rain.
I offer them cigarettes and we smoke, the smoke going out into
the rain, as if we're creating atmosphere for the memory archive.
Occasionally they mutter something in French, sort of shunting
the words in my direction. I piece together the best replies I can
manage, laugh a bit, wave my arms. Then one of them speaks in
English, asks me where I'm from. I tell them I'm from Liverpool
and they nod in approval. I'm hoping this is the way in for me to
get a swig of wine. They don't offer. The gutters are running with
muddy gluts of water the colour of milky coffee. One of the men
suggests perhaps that Reims is slowly sinking into the chalk and
clay of the terroir. He passes me the bottle, says it's champagne –
the finest champagne in Reims! It's gut rot but I gulp it down. So,
this is Reims – or that small part of Reims which is the doorway
of the Notre Dame Cathedral. I settle down on my duffle bag. We
pass the bottle. At some point in the early hours, while I've been
sleeping, the two men have wandered off, taking my Kodak camera
with them but leaving me the film.

I'm wet. The fear returns. I walk down the street until I see a
hotel where the receptionist is smoking in the doorway. I ask for
a room, and he wants paying upfront because he doesn't trust
me. I haven't got any money, so I show him my stash of traveller's
cheques and he lets me have a bed for the night but insists on
locking me in the room. Three hours later he unlocks the door,
takes me down to breakfast, watches over me suspiciously as I eat
the bread and cheese. And then, watching me closely, he walks me
up the street to a bank where I cash a cheque and pay him what I
owe. He counts the money, licking his finger, looking at me with
disdain. And then he leaves me there, counting the money again
as he walks back to the hotel.

The city is luminous in the morning light, a glycerin sheen on
the surface of the world as the limestone and clay slick begins to

dissolve in mist. It's beautiful. I walk the streets in a daze and sit in a cathedral pew in an almost religious state of ecstasy. Up above me in the cathedral heavens there are saints and angels. And then with sheer delight I realise I'm looking at stained glass windows designed by Marc Chagall – dream visions of Christ and Mary, illuminated by the morning sky. I almost say a prayer. Silence. And then I walk out of Reims, out into a country lane through fields of rising mist. It's time to go to Paris.

Kaleidoscope

L iverpool... the city is a memory archive and it's also an archive of the lost, a future archive of tomorrows. I love the way that cities are put together – this building against that building, this often-accidental arrangement, this atmosphere and shadow, this glimpse of that particular aspect, this forgotten corner, the light shining on the overlooked.

I walk down Huskisson Street in 2022 and stop at number 45. This is the house where the poet C. P. Cavafy lived. You can walk past it on your way to Peter Kavanagh's for a pint and probably wouldn't notice it. Why would you? On a row of Georgian houses, it looks no different to its neighbours. I think I used to come here for a pot of tea with friends; I don't think any of us knew that a poet had lived here, a genius. Although, in Liverpool, the odds are that a poet lived in every one of these houses. When I found out, years later, that Cavafy lived here when he was a child, the house was changed in my imagination forever. I can now see Cavafy looking out of an upstairs window in the 1870s, but I can't remember which friends of mine used to live here. I lived in Huskisson once, and Falkner, and the Square, and Sandon, and the Avenue, and Upper Parliament, and Catharine. I used to buy records off a man who lived on Huskisson, but I don't think it was this house. He'd open up his wardrobe and pull out vinyl he knew I'd like – Howlin' Wolf, Rahsaan Roland Kirk, Sleep John Estes, Donny Hathaway – and we'd listen to them on his old Dansette before I parted with a fiver per album and took them home like treasure. On my way to the pub to meet the poet Will Burns, I stop to pay homage to the poet Cavafy on the street where I used to see the poet Adrian Henri in the days when I lived on Falkner Square and was trying to be a poet. I know Cavafy's lines by heart: *The city will follow you. You will roam the same streets. And you will age in the same neighborhoods; in these same houses you will grow grey...*

On Moorfields, looking at anarchist stickers on lamp posts, I remember The Wizard's Den in a building that's no longer there where we used to buy Magic Water flower shells. We'd put them in a glass of water when we got home and watch them open, releasing a floating paper garden of delicate petals. This memory takes me into childhood, a conduit into the moment when my sister Val drops the seashell into the glass, watching closely as it opens up and the paper flowers unfurl. We are looking into a glass lagoon where pale petals shimmer in water. My sister's eyes are wide, the wonder of her gaze.

On Old Hall Street I watch myself aged eighteen leaving the office on a Friday afternoon, knowing I will never return. The walk is a séance. A summoning of spirits. A summoning of the ghost of myself. It reminds me of the days when I was 'loaned' to the post room and the old men who worked there – the Harrys and Berts who called everyone Bill or John – would send me out with a satchel full of letters and parcels which I had to deliver to other offices in other buildings. I'd climb the stairways and fire escapes I once climbed with my mum when we went for a nose. And after I'd emptied the satchel, I'd go to the pub for a secret pint. I'd sit in the Lion or the Pig and Whistle, playing truant from the office. Sometimes, I'd go up to the top floor of the multistorey car park and sit on the satchel with my back to the wall in the afternoon sun, looking up at the St Johns tower, watching its shadow turn like a sundial, seeing how long I could stretch time before my supervisor noticed I was missing.

★

In the museum aquarium, in the gloom of green and blue light,
we used to gaze in sadness at illuminated fish and two turtles we
wished we could release. I came here as a child and then later
with my friends and we'd tap gently on the glass, as if trying to
send messages to the creatures in the tanks. The museum building
was full of butterflies and spiders in chests of drawers and there
were Egyptian mummies in open caskets that used to fascinate
and terrify me all at once. But it was the subterranean aquarium
I loved and feared the most. It was a building with an ocean in
its basement, an ocean filled with iridescent angelfish and neon
tetras glinting in the dark.

On Pembroke Place I remember the lung machine. It was some
kind of public open day at the School of Tropical Medicine,
and my mum and I went up onto a rooftop where there were
greenhouses full of plants. In one greenhouse there were enormous
butterflies that landed on our fingers. We were nervous but tried
not to be. We blinked our eyes. And then we went to some kind
of laboratory where there was a glass tank, just like an aquarium,
and inside the tank there was an enormous piece of meat, as big as
a dog, and it was connected to tubes and a pumping machine that
made the meat breathe in and out and I realised it was a human
lung. I was frightened. And every time I walk down Pembroke
Place, I remember the lung machine.

I didn't know what the crematorium was, but I knew somehow
it was connected with uncles and grandparents, with people who
were no longer here. It was a silent playground where people
walked slowly and talked in hushed whispers while my mother
read the names of people etched into the walls and the petals of
dead flowers drifted over the flagstones. When we used to play
here after school, or sometimes on summer Sundays, we would
gather up the heads of roses dry as paper and place them in the

hands of stone angels. We were playing in a place where people become ash. Sometimes there would be cards and letters, blue ink handwriting blurred by rain. We would watch our mother bending down to read them, sometimes touch them, sometimes with moving lips. We didn't know she was talking to the dead.

When one of the warehouses on Jamaica Street was demolished and the fire-flowers bloomed, I climbed over the perimeter fence and walked through weeds. The dormant seeds of plants, buried under the building a hundred or more years ago, had been waiting for sunlight. Rosebay willow herb came back to life like Blitz flowers after the bombs. This was *actual regeneration*, rewilding as a spirit of natural resistance and resilience. One night I performed a magic ritual and wedged seeds and bird skulls into cracks in the wall of a new block of luxury apartments – a hex on brain-dead redevelopment, like placing cassettes of pagan information into the dead soul of a new building. Planting seeds.

There's a ghost sign on the side wall of a shop near where I live – an advert that once said SUNRAY but now says SUN RA. Sometimes the man who runs the secondhand shop paints over it, but the paint is soon washed off by the rain and SUN RA returns like a supernatural reminder that Herman Poole Mount, the cosmic jazz visitor from Saturn, once came to this city and tilted it off its axis. The presence of Sun Ra and his Arkestra in Liverpool was so potent that his essence seeped into the very fabric of the city. At least, that's the way I choose to see it. The night the Cosmic Love Arkestra played the Bluecoat Art Centre, on the 8th of June 1990, was an altered state event that made me think about the city differently. It made me imagine the city as a dream possibility. Whenever I go to the Bluecoat Chambers, I remember the music's spell. I can hear it. The music of Sun Ra has become part of the building. The moment the Arkestra walked on stage felt like a transformational jolt to my imagination. It was like the opening parade of a carnival, a wild cacophony of joyous mayhem. Here was music that conjured up delirium. The world was stranger, more mythic, more eccentric, more kaleidoscopic than you realised. In retrospect, that night, the way I felt, the synesthetic altered state changed the way I think about the world, animating my interpretation of the city as a living thing, a theatre, a circus. It happened when Captain Beefheart and the Magic Band played at Rotters Club and the city felt like one of his songs for days. It happened when Steve Reich played *Different Trains* at Edge Hill railway station and we stood there in the rain listening to the music ricocheting off the walls of the city. It happened when I lay down on the ground alongside Joseph Beuys's basalt slabs in the Tate gallery and believed I could hear tape loops playing inside the stones. Altered states. I walked through Liverpool after the Arkestra gig, and the music came with me. It seeped into the buildings. Sun Ra hadn't just changed my imagination. He'd also changed *the architecture.*

When I go to the Palm House in the park, I remember it when it was dying. When the glass skin was broken, and the skeleton of its glass lantern was twisting out of shape. For years, the melancholy spectre seemed to hang in the winter trees, abandoned and unwanted. I remember coming here with my grandad on the day we sailed my wooden yacht in the boating lake. I remember sitting on a bench in a shelter and being scared of dozens of daddy long legs as they crawled across the walls. And then we went to look at tropical palms in the sultry heat of this strange garden. When I go to the Palm House now, I remember my grandad's hand holding my hand, and in my other hand a wooden yacht. I remember glass and insects.

The buildings I remember and return to are recording devices, capturing and retaining memories like dreamcatchers. A building is a tape recorder. I sometimes think if you placed a stethoscope's resonator against the skin of a building you would hear its heart and the voices of the dead.

★

The photographs I took of buildings in Brussels, I never got developed. I don't know what happened to the film, at what point I lost it. Maybe I accidentally threw it away? Would I remember the trip to Paris differently if I still had the photographs? If I could take them out of my wallet and remind myself of the Atomium and the Grand Place and the mad, wayward adventure? The photographs are lost; whatever they captured, whatever they preserved was intended to be an aide to memory somewhere in the future. I couldn't contain the architecture in my head, the Grand Place's sheer *narcissism*. Photographs are evidence. Without them my remembering is improvised. Perhaps the photographs have carried on without me and they're remembering the past in a different way, sold on eBay or in a car boot sale, a collection of out-of-focus snapshots, anxiety Kodaks. A blurred shot of a woman wearing a piece of carpet as a cloak and offering me an egg.

Rue-Git-le-Coeur

I climb the Paris Metro stairs and emerge in Place St Michel on what might be Saturday night or might be a hallucination. The fountain on the square is full of bubbles, washing-up liquid frothing and floating across the square, clouds of soap-ghosts. Paris is the wrong colour! I'd imagined it to be pink and white like icing on wedding cakes, but it's drab brown and dull. I walk through crowds, wondering where to look for a bed for the night, thinking I'll sleep rough, thinking I'm too frightened to. And then I find myself following a tramp – another revenant, like Kerouac's dignified old bum in a full brown robe and grey beard like *an old member of the Syriac Church; either that or a Surrealist.* He's wearing a voluminous brown overcoat that scrapes the ground as he goes, as he bends to scoop up cigarette butts with dirty fingers. I walk a few paces behind him, follow him through an archway into a dirty alley and then he disappears like a shadow phantom. There's a hotel to the right, a bit of a dive, dimly lit, unwelcoming. So, of course, I go in and ask in my appalling French if they have a room. The receptionist laughs at me and slides the register across the counter. I pay up front for four nights and she gives me the key to a room on the top floor. I go upstairs, and as I get higher the carpeted stairs give way to bare boards and the landing on the top floor is covered in sheets of newspaper. There's a toilet to the left, a hole-in-the-floor latrine with a frosted glass window and the stink of upset stomachs. I open the door to my room. A huge cast iron bed with two fat eiderdowns. A window overlooking rooftops: chimney pots, smoke, dirty stairs, the sound of traffic and voices drifting in from the city. A wonky Van Gogh print of rooftops, just like the one pinned above a blocked sink with a wooden spoon on a chain (presumably to unblock it). I open the window and breathe the city in. Paris!

I got to Paris in three lifts. The first one was in a red sports car driven by a beautiful woman in her fifties – the sort of fantasy lift male hitchhikers talk about on motorway hard shoulders. She dropped me at a junction where she reckoned I stood more chance of making good distance. Straight away a van stopped – it looked like an enormous fridge on wheels. I got in the cabin; it stank of fish and so did the man and woman inside it. I offered them cigarettes; they offered me Fisherman's Lozenges. Fishmongers who eat themed lozenges! Married fishmongers and loud laughers. The man constantly wound down the window to spit, the woman knitted a scarf and sang. It was the best lift I'd had, and the maddest. They took me on their delivery round to farmhouses and village shops down winding country lanes. We stopped to talk to horses. At a run-down barn, a farm labourer paid for his fish with a live chicken, which joined us in the delivery truck. And then, in a café, with hugs and back slaps, they handed me over to the driver of a haulage truck who took me fifty miles. As he drove, he ripped into sugar sachets, pouring the entire contents into his mouth, babbling in his sugar rush, nostalgic for his years as an amateur boxer. I could feel Paris getting closer, feel the dream becoming real. He dropped me at the edge of the city and I remember feeling like I was in a film – a travelling man, a fugitive. I'm remembering that moment now, watching the film in my head, grainy footage daubed with night and weather, romanticised surveillance of a younger me, a bit more confident, a bit more alive, a bit more together, stepping down from the cab and swaggering off, bag slung over shoulder, into the big city. The reality is that I was some kind of idiot-innocent who stepped over the edge and lost his mind.

★

The revenant is singing in the alley, a sinister lullaby. The bed is rattling, its springs are poking through the mattress. I think the man is singing *A Flower is a Lovesome Thing*, Billy Strayhorn's achingly beautiful ballad, *Azaleas drinking pale moonbeams*. It feels like Robert Mitchum has strayed out of *The Night of the Hunter* and he's serenading me the night before he kills me in this bed. Through the window I can see Paris being Paris, the hum and murmur of it, the chimney-potted, higgledy-piggledy rooftop of sheer Parisian wonder. Feeling like Henry Miller in *Tropic of Cancer*, I go to sleep. An exhausted, nightmare sleep. In the morning I am covered in itchy red blotches, and I feel even more like Henry Miller because bedbugs have eaten me alive.

I get dressed, go downstairs, and when I get out in the alley I look up at the street name and realise by some strange chance I have arrived at a place I've read about in books. This is Rue-Git-Le-Coeur, and the hotel I'm staying in is across the road from the Beat Hotel. I feel like an accidental pilgrim who's arrived at his sacred destination. In this building, in the late 1950s, William Burroughs and Brion Gysin holed-up in an upstairs room in Mme Rachou's squalid, Class 13 dive, pages of *Naked Lunch* scattered across the mattress, bits of paper everywhere like ticker tape, sliced up with a Stanley blade; Allen Ginsberg and Sinclair Beiles, sifting through the pages; Gregory Corso writing *Bomb* and hustling for loose change and cigarettes; Burroughs, the waking cadaver, tapping away at his Underwood typewriter. It's all going on – Corso's *Gasoline* is ready to go, Ginsberg's *Kaddish* is pouring from his mind. Out of this rundown hotel in a dirty back alley, a new, delinquent literature crawled. The revenant had brought me here; I'm too frightened to knock on the door for fear of what might lurk inside. In any case, it looks closed, derelict, forgotten. I want to talk to someone about it, about all this, about the sheer *Parisness* of Paris. So I go looking for a bar.

★

The man who sits down next to me is too big for his clothes. The seams on his greasy suit are splitting to make room for his heavy-horse body. His cheap shoes are splitting too, open-mouthed. I notice this because he takes them off and shows me. I nod and sip my beer and hope he goes away. I open *The Mote in God's Eye* at a random page and pretend to read. I get stuck on the same sentence over and over again. *The scars of battle showed everywhere, ugly burns where the ship's protective Langston Field had overloaded momentarily…*

The haulking man is looking at my beer. He leans, 'So, this is where I say, "Nice day for it" and you reply, "Considering the time of year." Or some such.' His body spasms – sudden jolts of chaotic, hot-wired lurch and then a slumping back into his own gravity. He tells me he's hungover, hates Paris and would kill for a drink. I buy him a beer. He says he'd love to go to the pictures and his dentures are killing him. He speaks in random scraps of sense and nonsense and offers me his shaking hand. Swollen knuckles twisted and arthritic, blunt stabbers. This is Baxter, a Londoner in exile. He picks up *The Mote in God's Eye* and shoves it in his pocket. We drink two beers and then we go for a walk. He has a rough sense of what I'm interested in and every few paces he waves vaguely at a café or building and says: 'Here, you've got your Balzac… and over here you've got your de Beauvoir… and so on and so forth…' jabbing his thumb at doorways and pavement cafés like a tourist guide with amnesia and Tourette's.

Over the years, images from films, snatches of songs, paintings and photographs, sentences memorised from books had become an unreliable fantasy of a city I'd never visited, a sellotaped together hallucination-scrapbook. Here is Antoine Doinel in *The 400 Blows* playing truant, akin to Billy Casper, akin to Jamie in Bill Douglas's trilogy, *My Childhood, My Ain Folk* and *My Way Home*, stealing milk and running down the Montmartre streets carrying a typewriter; here is the Situationist graffiti *Beneath the paving stones, the beach!* daubed on brick; there is eight-year-old me, shaking a snow dome in Mrs Williams's front parlour on Winslow Street, the tiny Eiffel Tower inside it, pretty in the snow; Gene Kelly and Lesley Caron dancing on the banks of the Seine in *An American in Paris,* my mum swooning in delight on a Sunday afternoon, in the television glow; a photograph of Miles Davis, 'the Picasso of Jazz' and Juliette Greco in 1949, backstage at the Salle Pleyel – she's looking at his hands, his fingers pressing the valves of his trumpet, her own hands holding herself, holding her desire. Then a memory of the first time I read the opening words of *Tropic of Cancer,* that conjuring of bohemian squalor, of Paris exiles starving for their art, *I am living at the Villa Borghese. There is not a crumb of dirt anywhere, nor a chair misplaced. We are all alone here and we are dead*; Jeanne Moreau in *Jules et Jim,* singing Le Tourbillon, *She had eyes, eyes of oval...* On a postcard I used as a bookmark, the haloed moon of Chagall's *The Concert,* shining down on boating lovers, the hazy daub of the Eiffel Tower, like a memory erasing. None of this is the real Paris; all of this is the real Paris. The Paris I wanted to run away to and now I walk through it in tears.

On Boulevard de Clichy I look for Antoine Doinel, walking past the Wepler with his friend Rene, seeing his mother kissing her lover at the entrance to the Metro on Place Saint-Augustin. On Rue des Martyrs he's walking home from school with his mother, pausing outside the pâtisserie. I buy a croissant, imagining his shadow. Somewhere near here he plays pinball, jazz on a jukebox. And then my favourite scene – he rides The Rotor, the wooden cylindrical drum, pressing himself against the wall, hands in pockets, spinning as it rotates, faster and faster in a giddy blur, the screams of delight as people seem to levitate, weightless in the dizzy whizz and spin.

★

Maybe I came to Paris because I want to levitate and whirl and spin, to make more interesting memories than the ones I was accumulating in the council office, head full of minor anxieties and resentments, dread-thoughts, small mistakes, clock-watching hours, ploughman's lunches, bible-spouting supervisors, stealing pens from the stationery cupboard as the only relief from endless, dreary days. I had to get out of the office to rewire my brain. On the days when I'd go AWOL on the postal round, on the days when I phoned in sick, I'd walk around Liverpool just *absorbing* it, drinking it all in, almost as if it would disappear if I didn't keep looking at it closely, memorising the details of that building, the atmosphere of that alley. Watching the 'lifers' in the park aviary, the parrots that had seemingly been left behind in the semi-derelict cages, the mice scurrying in the dust for scraps of bread thrown there by pensioners. Looking for the site of the house where Margaret Ley the Castle Street Witch lived, dowsing for occult traces of her, somewhere in the ghost town. Searching for gallows sites, for the place where Patrick Byrne and Silvester Dowling were hanged in 1788, their dangling bodies watched by 15,000 people while touts roamed the crowd selling the broadside ballad, *The Sorrowful Lamentation*, written by the robbers in their prison cell.

> Farewell our friends, farewell our friends,
> And think of our untimely ends,
> Farewell our wives and children dear,
> Forget that ever we came here...

Sometimes I'd just look at mud and silt in the abandoned docks, or sit in pubs, and wonder what the fuck to do with today, tomorrow, and all the rest of it.

In Paris we stand, my new friend Baxter and I, looking at a goose in a cage, outside some kind of animal shop on the banks of the Seine. While I'm trying to get my head around the goose, Baxter is reading bits of *The Mote in God's Eye* out loud, as if reciting to the goose. He thinks I've given him the book as a gift. He doesn't want it. He spits the lines with contempt: *There was no Langston Field generator aboard the cutter, and no Alderson Drive… Jack Cargill remembered the speed with which the Motie had rebuilt his big percolator… It was unlikely that God had created beings with souls and no intelligence… they might even be a form of angel…* I laugh with embarrassment and say, 'I meant to bring Genet.'

We look in the windows of shops that sell fountain pens, broken dolls and puppets, meat, antique paper, jazz records, anatomy skeletons, wedding dresses, Turkish carpets, ink and paint made from wildflowers and insects, fairytale compendiums, inflatable dolls. It's like window shopping with Tom Waits. I am exhausted. He wants to keep walking. He suddenly wants a chocolate crêpe and asks if I have any money, and do I want to meet his wife and why don't we eat some oysters? We go into a brasserie, Café Wepler on Place de Clichy, where he swears we can buy absinthe. He knows the barman, who he says knew Henry Miller who used to drink here in the 1930s, where according to Miller (in 'Quiet Days in Clichy') …*the rosy glow which suffused the place emanated from the cluster of whores who usually congregated near the entrance. As they gradually distributed themselves among the clientele, the place became not only warm and rosy but fragrant. They fluttered about in the dimming light like perfumed fireflies.* Today there is hardly a soul in the place, no Miller, no Modigliani, no Truffaut or Claude Chabrol, just a cluster of businessmen eating omelettes and an old man furiously reading a newspaper and arguing with its pages. My new friend orders two green fairies and a plate of octopus, says the absinthe is an under-the-counter secret for those in the know. And when we drink, Baxter is immediately off his skull and spilling octopus down the napkin he has tucked into his vest, singing a murder ballad, *She walks these hills in a long black veil, she visits my grave when the night winds wail.* I feel like I've removed myself from everything I have previously known. I don't trust Baxter an inch. When he falls asleep I retrieve my book from his pocket, pay the bill and slip away. I walk. And the thought suddenly occurs to me – I'm having the time of my life.

The mystery of the next corner, that's what keeps me walking. Every time I turn, a new city reveals itself. I walk for hours through streets, through alleys and arcades. Twilight, somewhere on the Left Bank, looking for poets, for traces of ghosts in sulky rain. Everyone I came here looking for is long gone, most of them are dead. Beckett is still here, somewhere, writing himself into silence. George Whitman is still here in the shadows of his bookshop but I'm too shy to talk to him. I gaze into bars and cafés, but I don't go inside. I watch two small girls teaching each other dance steps, a pavement ballet school. I buy a Serge Gainsbourg postcard to use as a bookmark in the book I will buy tomorrow before I call it a day and head for home. And as I walk through Paris I think not of Paris but of Liverpool, and even though I tell myself I like feeling lonely, this is *too lonely* and I begin to cry.

The Zoo of Skylight

Most of the time you're surrounded by your own history. The place I wanted to be when I left home was a place where I had no past, no ancestors, no memory. Dislocation from the familiar. Absence. Erasure. The opposite of the way I think and feel now that I'm in my sixties – the past, my ancestors, memory are the centre of my being. These aren't things I actually thought at the time. I wasn't that aware of what I was doing, but looking back, this must have been my unconscious motivation. Some kind of half-arsed self-annihilation, just to get away from myself, without a thought, to rip it up and start again. I walked through Paris for hours and got so lost that it didn't matter anymore. Often, when people arrive in a new place, they say they felt instantly at home. I didn't want to feel at home. I wanted to have that feeling of uncertainty, of being unsettled, the uncertainty I kept returning to for years. I wanted to feel as if I had no skin.

Now I look into shadows, at my father, in the past. He's a fourteen-year-old and he's underground. The shelters on Sheil Road have been abandoned now that the war is over. There are bunk beds and sleeping cots and he is dismantling them with a claw hammer. When he emerges from the shelter, he is carrying bundles of wood over his shoulder, tied together with lengths of cable. There are pieces missing from the city – places that were once familiar, but they have been obliterated by bombs. Erased. He walks through rubble and empty spaces where there used to be buildings. I can see him, the skinny kid, slowly walking through the devastation, pitching up at houses and rattling the door knocker, asking the women who open the door if they want to buy any firewood. Stashing his spoils in grandad's back yard and wandering through the bombsites, the demented playground. During the Blitz when he climbed up through the skylight onto the roof, he was the watcher of the skies, the overseer of oblivion. He had first-hand knowledge of a place being there, and then not being there, of a thing you know being present and then becoming absent. He was a witness to erasure and the aftermath of absence. He used to tell the stories, his repertoire of stories. He doesn't tell the stories anymore.

In the attic of our house on Winslow Street, in the shadow of Everton's ground, my sister Val and I built a zoo. The people who lived in the house before us had left behind a homing pigeon cage. It was full of shredded paper, and we cleared little spaces in the straw, sort of trampling it down with our hands. In each space we placed a plastic or wooden animal until the cage was full of beasts – a crocodile, an elephant, a lion and a seal, and there were farm animals, including a plastic piggy bank with a rip in its back where I'd sliced into it to get the money out. It was the Zoo of Skylight. Twice a day we'd climb the wooden stairs to the zoo to feed the animals on raisins and currants, and we'd top up the water bowl where the seal swam. On one occasion there was a royal visit and my sister dressed up in mum's wedding dress, making a very grand entrance and marvelling at the splendid zoological display. After a while, our dad closed down the zoo because he was worried the raisins and currants would attract mice, and after that the attic became a royal palace.

There is a sweet-light glimmer to these memories of the attic zoo and palace, of the ways we transformed the wooden room into imaginary places, the way the sun slanted in through the skylight, and the way the roar of the Wednesday night football crowd seemed to roll over the rooftop and flood the attic with songs. I wanted to climb out through the skylight the way my dad had done during the Blitz. I wanted there to be a war so I could lie on the slates and count the Heinkels in the sky. The sky would be a great adventure, even greater than the palace and the zoo.

One night the house was full of firemen because the chimney had caught fire. We sat there in our pyjamas while men in yellow trousers dragged hosepipes from the street into the parlour and dowsed the flames. The house filled with the smell of wet ash and soot and the men ruffled our hair. Our mum made cups of tea and dad put newspaper down on the linoleum to soak up the pools of water. There was smoke in the house and in our pyjamas. It was exciting, like a war. I had imagined an inferno so vividly that it came true.

Proxima Centauri

There is no mirror. I do not shave. There is no shower. The sink is blocked with matted hair. I do not wash. I do not comb my hair. The shared-hole-in-the-floor toilet on the landing makes me gag. I lie in bed, eating bread and oranges. At night the revenant sings, his voice smoking up from the alley. The mattress is the breeding ground for all the fleas in Paris. But just look at that view across the rooftops – it keeps making me cry. Dreams arise from dust, through the window the sky is full of lovers, men and women dancing in the heavens, dreams painted by Marc Chagall. Andromeda and the Milky Way – like my mum's pyjamas – shimmer in the city-glow. Antoine Doinel, Truffaut's truant, is running through the alleyways of shadowplay night.

Be not inhospitable to strangers, lest they be angels in disguise... I stand in the beautiful half-light of Shakespeare and Company bookshop, and I want to pluck up the courage to ask for a job, to ask if I can live there for a while. I can't ask the question – an eternal regret. I spend hours skulking in the upstairs rooms, opening books, reading fragments. I buy a battered copy of Rimbaud's *Illuminations* and slip my Serge Gainsbourg postcard between its pages. Years later, in 2002, I will sit upstairs with George Whitman, the legendary proprietor of the legendary bookshop. We will drink dry sherry at breakfast time and talk about Beat poetry and absinthe for a programme I am making for BBC radio about this very trip to Paris in the 1970s. He will show me one of the rooms where I might have slept, if I'd plucked up the nerve. At George's invitation I will lie down on the overstuffed bed and try it out for size. He will tell me that I could have been a tumbleweed, slept in that bed and read a book a day. And later in my hotel room, I will sit and listen to the exiled poet Gerald Mangan read his versions of Arthur Rimbaud's poems in his beautiful Glaswegian accent, swigging lemonade from the bottle between stanzas, wild haired, gentle soul. The absintheur Peter Shaff will visit, carrying his cooler box full of ice and spirits. We will drink absinthe together, beginning with a tiny blue bottle of 100-year-old *la fee verte* he discovered behind a bar in Corsica, fragrant with sweet fennel and artemisia. And I will fall backwards through time, to the 1970s, to the day I wished I could be a tumbleweed, to the Paris of my disappearing days.

I have been to look at water lilies. I don't know how long I stood in front of Monet's paintings, just trying to understand what I was seeing, what I was feeling. I'd only ever seen these flowers on postcards and Athena posters. Expecting quiet contemplation and a feeling of soporific tranquillity, my experience was the exact opposite, possibly because I was hot-wired to the moon. Immersed in painted marks and daubs and murk I felt like I was drowning, voluntarily submitting to aqueous hallucinations. I stood there, thinking of Monet's cataracts, his near blindness, his proximity to death. Immersed in this unsettling but beautiful dream I closed my eyes, and the paintings were still there on my eyelids. I had entered the paintings, or the paintings had entered me. After a while, needing to steady myself, feeling tears welling up in my eyes, I left the gallery. I remember consciously thinking this: *I think I'm breaking down.* I hadn't eaten properly for days. I hadn't changed my clothes or shaved. Suddenly frightened and desperately lonely, I went to a bar in the Marais, and it was at this point I knew for certain it was time to go home. I had run out of detonators – those solar flares in the head, the sparks, the mechanisms that set the fuse burning and drive you on through anxiety and fear. Sitting on the terrace over the dregs of my beer, I closed my eyes and could see water lilies. Eyelids full of flowers.

In bed, beneath my eiderdown quilts, I count my money. I'm running out. I get out of bed and leave the hotel. The revenant is leaning against a wall. I give him some coins, as if giving him a tip for his lullabies. I walk to the Gare du Nord, buy a train and ferry ticket to London Victoria three days from now. I write a postcard to my parents, *I think I might come home...* I walk back to my room down Rue St. Denis, pass sex shops, prostitutes in doorways, *Tropic of Cancer* atmospheres, noir shadows, Willie Ronis photographs brought to life, the city's underbelly. Back in my room I climb into bed. To this day, whenever I think of Paris I immediately think of that bed – its eiderdowns, its view across the rooftops, the smell of the drains. I think of my head opening up. I think of some kind of minor madness and bedbugs eating me alive. I count my money again. I'm broke, but not quite as broke as I thought. I say out loud, *I'm going to go on holiday.*

I stick to the backstreets mostly, the bruised and shabby places where there is hardly ever sunlight. I like the network of drab, narrow streets around Rue St Denis, the strangely silent hinter, clogged gutters and abandoned fruit crates, dust. I find these fugitive alleys more *Parisian* than the rest of the city. I like the steamy smell of launderettes, the glimpses of mechanics tinkering with machines, the smokers leaning out of upstairs windows. Streets that smell of petrol and cigarettes and meat. There is an old woman with a coat made of blankets. A boy chalking dogs on the pavement with a stone. In a corner bar, drinking at the zinc, there are two butchers with identical moustaches, nodding up at a football game on a faulty television. Up above the doorway in a cage, a chaffinch. In the gutter in a nest of tissue paper there are two bruised apples. I pick them up, pocket one and eat the other, swallowing the pips. Nothing here is beautiful in the accepted sense, but I don't want to leave. These streets feel as if they have quietly shrugged off *that* Paris and become the streets they wanted to be.

I go to graveyards. I touch the tombs of Oscar Wilde, Apollinaire and Edith Piaf. I steal a cork from Jim Morrison's grave. I browse in the Bouquinistes on the banks of the Seine. I sit on a bench at the Eiffel Tower watching skateboarders. I eat crêpes in the Luxembourg Gardens, sitting on a bench in spring sunshine watching nannies pushing prams and old men playing boules. It's finally spring, and as I sit on the bench my anxiety fades. I stand outside Samuel Beckett's apartment on rue de la Grande Chaumiere, hoping to catch a glimpse of him, perhaps follow him to a brasserie. In the dark, I gaze up at Notre Dame. It looks like a skull, cathedral anatomy, haunted and mournful. I sit in a café on Place St Michel just watching, looking at Paris. I buy a notebook and write it all down, *I am in Paris...* I wish I still had the notebook. I go to the cinema. I sit there in the dark, watching *The Wizard of Oz* and surreptitiously eating chunks of bread and chocolate. I feel like a child. I like the feeling. Dorothy is dancing. The wicked witch is dead. I remember acting out the film with my sister Val at home in the garage – I am the witch, and she is Dorothy. My broom is a broken umbrella. The garage is in Technicolor. I come out of the cinema and walk along the river. On the Pont Neuf I bump into Baxter. He's looking at the stars. He invents some galaxy knowledge and delivers it like a deranged astronomer. 'Your Proxima Centauri over here, the vast eternal cosmos in the glimmer of God's eyeball, and so on and so forth.' He suggests we go and look at the goose again, perhaps we can set it free, which makes me laugh. Instead, we go to a bar in the Latin Quarter and wait for his wife. He doesn't know how long he's been in Paris, came here for a fortnight, stayed at least ten years. Does a bit of this, a bit of that, drinks too much, is 'clean from the needle', thinks he might be in his 50s. His wife is like a decaying Simone Signoret. She's English but she has a touch of the Saint-Germain-des-Prés artist about her. Faded glamour with cigarette stains on her teeth, cackle laughter. Baxter is already drunk. My notebook is on the table. He reaches for it and starts reading bits of it to his wife, laughing at my stumbling attempts at the poetic. Embarrassed, I grab hold of my book, down my drink and head out into the street, his laughter coming after me.

On my last day in Paris I get up early, pack my duffle bag and walk to the train station where I take a seat in a waiting room full of people who have lost their way in life. There's a man in an overcoat that rattles when he shuffles up and down the room, demented whimpers coming out of him, some kind of song only he knows. Instead of shoes, he has tied stacks of cardboard and polystyrene to the soles of his feet with lengths of string and ribbon. There are young men who look like pickpockets, shifty-eyed loiterers, waiting for their moment. There must be twenty people here and all of them are desperate. They look as though they live here. There's an old woman, tiny boned, almost bald. She has folded herself into a corner, head tilted to the ceiling lights and occasionally she shouts out curses in a voice that sounds like a blues singer, broken and scratched. I'm too tired to walk any more so I've come here to wait eight hours for my train to Calais. I have no food, nothing to drink. I sit and read – attempt to read – *The Mote in God's Eye.*

An hour before the train is due to leave, I see Baxter standing in the waiting room doorway. He nods at me, beckons me to go over. Reluctantly I go to him, say hello. 'Not leaving, are you? Listen, we should have a coffee, maybe a sandwich, I know a place.' To this day I don't know why I agree to this, but I get my bag and we leave the station together, cross the road and go into a café. Two coffees, two cheese baguettes, he's paying. I tell him I'm going home, I've had enough. I'm homesick. 'Don't even think about it.' He leans into me, and I can smell beer, cigarettes, halitosis. 'I don't live far from here, you should come back to my place. I've got wine, marijuana, it could be fun. I'll phone my wife and tell her we're coming.' He goes to the phone booth, and I grab my bag and start to leave but he sees me sneaking out and follows me as I cross the road back to the station. He's so close he's almost tripping me up, perhaps he means to trip me up, I stumble as I hurry. He's shouting at me: 'I want my book back. You stole my *Mote in God's Eye!*' I tell him it's *my* book. I don't even want the book. I hate the fucking book. Just by the urinals, near the station entrance, he bundles me against the wall, pinning me, hand grabbing my throat, face up close to my face, breathing on me, a heavy heat. 'You fucker. Pathetic little fucker. Running away, is it? And so on and so forth? Come with me.' I push him away, heading for the platform. At the entrance to the metro, he vaults the gate, stands on the other side. He's beckoning me to go with him. 'A little drink then. I'll see you right!' He's shouting after me as I hurry away, growing fury in his voice. 'I bought you a coffee. I bought you a fucking sandwich! I showed you the sights.' I laugh and shout back at him, 'You showed me a goose in a cage! A fucking goose, dying in a cage!' I wave goodbye, laughing, frightened, run down the platform. I get on the train. Goodbye to Paris.

On the newsstand in Victoria Station, I read the papers. On the front page of one paper there's a story about backpackers going missing in Paris, last seen in the Gare du Nord. Fifteen people have gone missing in the last twelve months. I think of Baxter calling me, *Come with me... come with me...* I think I might have died.

I buy a ticket for the night bus back to Liverpool and spend the day in London splashing the last of my money on secondhand records in Cheapo Cheapo – Sly and the Family Stone's *There's a Riot Goin' On* and Can's *Soon Over Babaluma*. Transformational sonic magic to mark the end of the trip and take me into the uncertain tomorrow. I sleep in pale spring sunshine on the grass at Marble Arch, jagged dreams of broken endings flowing through my head. I dip my feet into the ice-cold water feature, the shock of the cold like needles in my blisters. And then I go to a phone booth and phone my parents. My mum's voice is like a choir-singer. She wants to know where I am and what my plans are. I tell her I'm in London. I'm coming home.

away into the ... city, silent phantom.

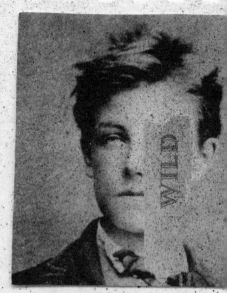

WILD

FERAL

WILLS'S CIGARETTES.

BLACKBIRD

LOST

CREYRFA = HERONRY

Family *ARDEIDÆ* = Herons

HERON = *CAYR GLAS*.   Length 37 in.

Ardea cinerea cinerea Linn.

The Heron is a beautiful waterbird, often standing motionless for a long time in shallow water watching for fish and frogs. One which I saw standing in a marsh, with its body hidden in reeds, was almost invisible; the long, snaky neck and thin, wedge-shaped head appearing to be only a whitened branch, until a slight movement betrayed it. When it takes to its great grey wings with dark tips, the unusually slow and languid wing-beats are distinctive. The usual position when standing is with the head sunk on the shoulders. The head is also drawn back in flight.

HAUNT. Marshes, woods, rivers, lakes, estuaries

NEST Of sticks, very large, usually in a tree, in a colony or heronry, sometimes in a marsh or on a cliff.

EGGS. 3 to 5, greenish-blue. February or March.

FOOD Fish, frogs, eels, insects, water-voles, and occasionally waterfowl, though nearly always young ones

NOTES. A sonorous "croak"

FEAR

WEATHE

Part Two

The memory is not what you remember:
the memory lies further down, or what, or whatever.

M. John Harrison, 'Wish I Was Here'

Mangled Cassette

On the way to the dole office the bus I'm on runs over a dog. I've been home a week, mostly asleep in bed, and when I finally manage to crawl out from my pit it's because I need free money. The bus jolts up into the air and then down again. The driver slams on the brakes and sits with his head in his hands. An old woman stands up and starts shouting at him and he tells her to fuck off. People gather around the bus and start banging on the door and windows. The driver forces a laugh – *It's only a stray dog!* – but you can tell he's sick to his stomach. The driver doesn't get out to check on the dog. None of us do. We're ashamed that we were somehow part of the killing. The bus moves off and we all sit there in shock. I look back down the road. The dead dog is lying in the gutter, and a man is checking if it's dead by prodding it with his foot. I get off the bus at The White Horse and walk to the dole office, shaken. When I ring the bell at reception, Stan comes to the desk, *How can I help you?* And then he looks up and sees it's me and the colour drains out of him, as if he's seen a ghost. He processes my claim, nervously, and tells me I'm not entitled to unemployment benefit because I walked out of my last job unannounced. Then he slips me a fiver and tells me to meet him in the White Horse when he's clocked-off from work.

I sit in the pub, nursing a brown bitter and at ten past five he joins me, sheepish. I ask him what the hell all that was about and he looks sideways to avoid eye contact, then tells me he only took two weeks annual leave and had never intended to go away for longer. *He never intended to follow the dream.* He makes me sick. I can hardly look at him. But, eventually, not knowing what to say or think, we're just two young men, drinking and rubbing along as best we can. On the bus home I pass the spot where the driver killed the dog. Someone's dumped its corpse on a patch of scrub beneath a hoarding. Standing over its body there's another dog, howling like a mourning widow. At home, Mum tells me she always knew Stan wasn't with me on the trip because she'd seen him at the shops the week after I left. We both laugh. It's so ridiculous, even my dad laughs too. I tell them I feel like a failure. *You didn't fail, you followed your heart.* We eat apple crumble. We watch *Starsky and Hutch.* I go to bed and listen to John Peel, recording him on cheap cassettes. I sleep.

Sometimes I go with my dad to the car auctions where he buys Austin Maxis for thirty quid. When the MOT is due he sells them for scrap – for thirty quid – and buys another one. We also go to the wholesalers on Kempston Street and buy novelty goods. On the night shift in the factory, he sets up a stall on a pasting table and sells cheap toys, playing cards, pencil sets, disposable razors. In the winter he sells snorkel jackets, and all the men in work go to union meetings dressed exactly the same. On Tuesdays and Fridays, we go to auction rooms and buy job-lots of kitchen stuff, house clearance crap. All his life he's done this – from the air raid shelter firewood bundles to the bags of sweets we weigh out on the kitchen scales – the Everton mints and fireman's hoses, the Sherbet Dabs and liquorice. When he was courting my mum, my nana warned her not to marry him because he'd keep coming home with all kinds of stuff nobody wanted. Sure enough, soon after the marriage, he came home from an auction sale with a leather suitcase full of loose buttons. My mum cried, thinking *Nana was right.* He tipped the buttons out on the kitchen floor and started sorting and threading them into sets with lengths of cotton, and then went out with the suitcase full of buttons, selling them from door to door. When he'd sold the last set, he sold the leather suitcase.

When I was still at school I knew a boy who kept tropical fish in tanks stacked up in his dad's garage. He lived just down the road from a boy who had an oscilloscope in his bedroom, and not far away from a girl who played woodwind instruments and was so clever she sat the entrance exam for Oxford University when she was fifteen. And in a rambling ruin of a house across the road, there was a boy who customised his bikes by fashioning handlebars out of car exhaust pipes. I wanted to be all of these children because they were strange and exotic creatures. The boy who kept tropical fish used to especially fascinate me because he wanted to be violent like the boys in skinhead gangs, but wasn't very strong. He had the clothes for it – two-tone trousers, the Astronaut boots, Ben Sherman shirts – but just didn't have the muscle or the fighting spirit, so he would often get his head kicked in by Spacey Moon and the other mad bastards who terrorised the streets. Sometimes I would go to his house and look at the tropical fish, and it was like a miniature version of the museum aquarium, a dark place full of tiny glinting lights in blue and green water. One day his father decided it was time for the fish to go. He wanted the garage back for a new car he had bought, and so some of the fish ended up in the aquarium outside the headmaster's office. The Jack Dempsey – an ugly-faced fish, a fish that ate other fish until it was the only fish left in the tank – attacked its own reflection in the glass until it died. The boy wasn't that bothered at first, but after a while I think the sadness got to him and he degenerated into a flotsam, submarine-version of himself, and eventually disappeared into whatever life he went on to live. The thing is, I've never forgotten him. And I've never forgotten the other exotic creatures who lived nearby. I've never forgotten how much I wanted to be like them, to be as strange and exotic as they were, to be different from the rest. Going to Paris – Paris the long way around – was probably my attempt to be different from the rest. And because I felt as though I'd failed, I began to disintegrate. In the weeks and months after I returned, I began to fall apart. Then one afternoon, while they were sitting in the garden, I overheard Mum say to Dad, *Maybe, if you spent more time with him? Ask him how he's feeling?* It was a prompt, rather than a suggestion, to find out why I was breaking apart.

I was curious about my loneliness. Even though I had a small group of close friends, I always felt alone. The thing is, I actually *liked* it, even cultivated it. You could go places in your own loneliness that you couldn't go when you were with other people. But also, you could be with other people and still be in that place, alone. You could disappear into the fiction of yourself, or into the alternative reality of your own mental theatre. It was stranger than oscilloscopes and Jack Dempsey fish.

Underneath the railway bridge, sometimes with my mate Pete, sometimes by myself, I'd smoke badly rolled spliffs and watch the trains roll by. Pete had a really good overcoat and records by German bands like Cluster, but because he was still at school, I had the days to myself. *He spends too much time alone,* I'd overhear my mum say to my dad. *You spend too much time alone,* she'd say to me. In the car driving into town one day my dad looked at me sideways and said, *Your mum thinks you spend too much time alone.*

In Liverpool, my friends and I walk the city – listening to Bible-bashing doom-prophets calling for the end times; looking for Cherry Blossom (AKA Boot Polish Head), the man who paints pretend hair on his skull with shoe polish; raiding abandoned warehouses and salvaging mooring ropes and dockers hooks; talking to No Smoking Man as he stands before his bicycle decorated with anti-tobacco slogans like an outsider artist protest;

standing on Bold Street, listening to the Picasso Sisters play their Scouse vaudevillian rags before they get arrested; trespassing in the Albert Docks when only the likes of Arthur Dooley could see they were worth saving; drinking in old men's pubs and wine lodges, slow dancing with old dears you've seen howling at the wrestling; crowding into the Metro cellar on Sweeting Street to watch Deaf School play – art school noir-chanson, bittersweet night songs – feeling like you were in on a wondrous secret. We walk the city, my friends and I, desperate to be part of its mythology.

I lie in bed repairing the cassette of *Marquee Moon* my friend Mark recorded off John Peel's radio show. It'd got mangled in the machine and I was turning the sprocket with a pencil, slowly winding the crumpled tape back into its case. Later, in the dark of Mark's bedroom, we hear a distant music, strange ether-signals, secret messages, beautiful Morse Code, *I remember how the darkness doubled, I recall, lightning struck itself, I was listening, listening to the rain, I was hearing, hearing something else.*

We get our information from paperbacks and records. The aura of particular books is palpable. You just *know* when you hold it in your hand that Kenneth Patchen's *The Journal of Albion Moonlight* is going to unbalance your imagination, somehow change you. Even if – especially if – you didn't understand it. *A child stands on the road watching us; upon her forehead is the yellow brand of this plague summer.* Uncertainty is part of the attraction. Tom Pickard's *Guttersnipe*, his 'apprentice novel', picked up in Out of Print on Renshaw Street, is uncouth and dirty and I carry it around and read it in pubs. In an auction sale job lot, my dad finds a first edition of Alexander Trocchi's *Cain's Book* and gives it to me saying, *I think this might be your kind of thing.*

★

I bought George Melly's *Revolt into Style* and Jeff Nuttall's *Bomb Culture* in Philip, Son & Nephew. They felt like temperature gauges, ways into secret knowledge. The Melly book is a portal into ideas about revolt. It confirmed the idea that Liverpool 8 is – or was – *a colony of native artists, musicians, poets and layabouts.* It made me even more convinced that I had to go and live there, a Scouse Greenwich Village, a Liverpool Scene. Prompted by Melly I read Sean Hignett's *A Picture to Hang on the Wall* and *All Night Stand* by Thom Keyes, hoping for maps into a Liverpool beatnik *demi-monde.* The pubs and clubs and streets were there – the Cracke, The Iron Door, Hope Hall, Falkner Square, Gambier Terrace – but the books themselves didn't have the wild energy and magic I was looking for. George Melly was looking for Liverpool's *Absolute Beginners,* but nobody had written it and there's still no sign of it being written. Sometime in the 1980s, when I lived in Falkner Square, I got drunk with Jeff Nuttall on elderberry wine in the Everyman Bistro and the Cracke. The night culminated in him having a fist fight with a drinker who had called Nuttall a cunt. Nuttall battered him. The next day in the Cracke, he was sitting on a barstool doing *The Times* crossword and he had no memory of the fight or of ever meeting me. When I met George Melly around the same time, he was dressed in a lilac, striped zoot suit and fedora, eating a bowl of sardines in Keith's Wine Bar on Lark Lane. These streets were his childhood territory. *Revolt into Style* became a guidebook to sacred monsters and awkward bastards. I read Stanley Reynolds in *The Guardian*, a Liverpool-based denizen of the low life zones whose 'Museum of the Horrifying Example' article, decrying the destruction of Liverpool's soul, thrilled and appalled me at once. Ray Gosling, Violette Leduc, Heathcote Williams, Michael Horowitz's *Children of Albion,* B. S. Johnson's *Albert Angelo* with the holes cut in the pages, picked up for a quid on Belmont Road market. I don't know what they are, don't quite understand them, but I buy them because they feel *dangerous and strange.* Solar flares. Nervous systems. It happens with Lou Reed's

Transformer – *I watched things for a little while, I like to watch things on TV*; Anna Kavan's *Ice* – *there was no time to lose, I was wasting time; it was a race between me and the ice.* Roxy Music's *Virginia Plain* – *take me on a rollercoaster, take me for an airplane ride*; Henry Miller's *Tropic of Cancer* – *we are all alone here and we are dead;* David Bowie on Top of the Pops – *didn't know what time it was, the lights were low oh oh;* Patti Smith's *Gloria* – *Jesus died for somebody's sins but not mine.* All of these were detonations. Fire alarms. Books and records trembling in your hands.

And then, in some kind of cancellation of myself, I went suddenly, abruptly, to Germany to have some kind of breakdown. Complete dislocation. Even though I liked the Liverpool drift, I wanted to get back to Europe. And so without really thinking about it, I answered an ad I saw in the paper. I didn't really want to, but I took a bar job on an army camp in Paderborn. Apart from my family and one or two friends, I didn't tell people what I was doing or where I was going. There was violence there, on a nightly basis. I drank until I was ill. I was desperately homesick.

In the wardrobe of my room in a shared flat, I found a box of records left by the man who was the barman before me, but he had to leave because he'd gone mad. I opened the box, and it was full of LPs by Amon Düül, Tangerine Dream, Neu, Agitation Free, Cluster. The man I shared the flat with owned one LP by the Commodores and he played *Once, Twice, Three Times A Lady* on repeat, singing along out of tune. The Irish Hussars who drank in the bar would only listen to Don Williams. They would sing along to *'Til the Rivers All Run Dry* and cry into their beers. Every night they'd link together the ring-pulls off their lager cans and make a metal curtain across the front of the bar. I'd have to part the curtains to pass them their drinks. At the end of every shift, I'd dismantle the curtain and the next night it would start all over again.

★

After work each night I'd go out drinking with my flatmate and other lost souls from England. Sometimes we'd get beaten up by squaddies, but we knew we had an advantage because if they were caught fighting in the town, the soldiers would end up in the slammer. We'd taunt them, push things as far as we dared. They'd chase us in their souped-up cars and give us a few slaps around the head in the underpass. I only realised how far I'd descended into some kind of mental illness after a night out with Ravin' Rupert, the Elvis Presley tribute act. My flatmate found me singing Don Williams songs to a mannequin in a department store shop window, *'Til the rivers all run dry, 'Til the sun falls from the sky, 'Til life on earth is through, I'll be needing you.*

In my first month in the job I worked 31 shifts on the go, and by the end of it, all I was fit for was bed. I'd lie beneath the sheets listening to Amon Düül and drinking Apfelkorn until I was sick. Out of my bedroom window, one night during an ice storm, I watched a drunk man crawling down the street on his hands and knees because the ground was so treacherous. Cars slipped and slid in slow motion, bumper kissing bumper. The crawling man met another crawling man and they held onto each other as they slid down onto their backs – just laying there on the ice, sliding slowly sideways, like two men on a moving, frozen bed. The whole scene was like a ballet, a silent opera. It made me cry. At Christmas, when I got fired for stealing from the till, I bought my mum a cuckoo clock and carried it home to Liverpool in a bin bag, along with the Amon Düül, Tangerine Dream, Neu, Agitation Free, and Cluster records. She hung the clock in the hallway and for years it cuckooed every fifteen minutes until it died. She'd tell visitors – or I imagined her telling visitors – she didn't really like it, but she wanted to make me happy. Listening to the cuckoo became a way for her to say, *You will be okay.*

★

Grandparents are dying in these years, fault lines are opening in the day to day, in the quiet lives of my parents. Sometimes my mother cries, a kind of loneliness because she's now an orphan. No one really talks about the deaths but there are sighs, and whispers and closed doors. My sister Val and I overhear quiet words of comfort. It's as if death has come to live with us even though the dead have gone away. The sounds of the house have changed, as if the sounds are fading light.

I have a memory of tiny diamonds of rainbow lights spinning across the walls of the room. My dad is holding a cut-glass bowl, turning it slowly in his hands, looking over the rim of his specs and weighing up the beauty of the object as it catches a sunbeam from the garden and sends shards of colour dancing around the house, a kaleidoscope of rainbows. Just watching him is beautiful. He's in a state of peaceful contemplation, and when he taps his fingernail against the glass it rings like a bell – or perhaps, almost like a crystal voice – which makes him smile. The glass is singing.

Around about this time, just like I had done with my childhood Airfix models, I burned the mangled cassettes in a garden bonfire. Marquee Moon, John Peel, Top of the Pops recordings, melting in the ashes. Magnetic-coated ribbons twisting into evening air, burning, floating. It was such a beautiful sight.

Roaming Stranger

In this downward spiral I met a woman called Becks at a bedsit party in Waterloo, North Liverpool. She was like a punk Elizabeth Taylor and between her eyebrows there was a fading scar from a pub brawl where she'd been glassed by a drunk speed freak – a scar like a kiss on a love letter. She arrived at the party with bruised knees after falling from her bicycle, but she didn't seem at all perturbed, perhaps because she was drunk on her favourite concoction of Merrydown Cider and Cinzano, a dash of Night Nurse on the top just to jazz things up a bit. Her dress was a customised priest's cassock, her hair tied back with a length of tinsel. It was love at first sight.

Because I'd travelled a bit, because she wanted to, there were lots of things to talk about, and she liked sitting in daytime pubs and walking on the promenade in winter. One morning, we broke off shards of ice from the edge of the water where the river meets the sea and skimmed them across the undulating surface, black triangles spinning into the darkness. There was always a stolen nail varnish clinking in her pocket, and she got tip-offs from old ladies in charity shops when a Biba piece, or a Mary Quant had been donated. The best music venue in town was the punk club Eric's where she had been the cloakroom girl. She knew the faces on the scene, dressed like a glamorous ragamuffin, but now she was a telephone operator and hated it. She couldn't wait to get away, to see the world. So we went travelling in Europe, thumbing it from Ostend to Italy, and then across to Athens and the Cyclades.

★

In Piraeus, she had a hissing fight with a cleaner and we slept on the harbour side, watching rats climb the mooring ropes of ships. In a two-quid-a-night room in Naxos, I started to feel ill – my lungs were closing down, until it was so painful to breath I couldn't speak. And then my joints seized up, my tongue swelled up, my balance and coordination went haywire, and the headaches were so intense that I couldn't raise my head off the pillow. Soaking wet with sweat, I slept for three days solid, and when I woke up the room was full of wildflowers and Becks was sitting there drinking Metaxa from a tin cup. I tried walking and could only walk a few steps at a time with Becks to hold onto. We had no travel insurance but a pharmacist agreed to examine me and concluded I had a throat infection – he gave me a pack of painkillers. We got the next ferry back to Athens where we slept on a rooftop – I don't know how many days – until I was ready to get a train heading north. The Acropolis Express. I think it took two days to get to Innsbruck, hot days and nights crammed in a sleeping compartment with four Norwegian women who ate watermelons and spat the pips out the window. The whole trip was a hallucinatory nightmare and we both thought I was dying. The Norwegian women thought so too, watching me with disgust as I sweated and shivered and held my head in pain. Throughout all this, Becks took care of me. She was kind and patient, checking my temperature, checking if I was dead or alive. In Hamburg, we slept in a cinema through three screenings of *A Clockwork Orange* dubbed into German. And then, because my boots were broken, we took it as a good omen when Becks found a pair of hiking boots next to a bin in the Reeperbahn. 'These boots are our good fortune,' she said, smiling. In Amsterdam we went to see a doctor, a specialist to people working on the black economy. He told me I had Guillain-Barré syndrome, and I was lucky to be alive.

★

Antibodies attack the nerves, the immune system is in revolt, the nerves become so damaged that the body becomes confused and goes to war against itself, against you. Holed up in a room, in my hallucinatory state, I veer between thinking this is either a healing ritual, a psychic attack, or an exorcism. It's like a psychotropic body and mind storm, a breaking open of my head and bones. For some inexplicable reason we go out one night to De Kroeg to see Louisiana Red. I manage to walk there but every time we cross a canal bridge, the effort of ascending and then descending the shallow incline is crippling. There are only about twenty people in the club. Becks and I stand close to the stage, the vibrations from the amps hitting me in the lungs and throat, pushing me against the walls where I slide down to the floor in a heap, *I'm a Roaming Stranger* pummelling my body. Tears streaming down my face, I can't get back on my feet unaided, so Becks and the doorman pull me up and load me into a taxi.

An Amsterdam night, stars the colour of Lucozade, glimpsed through rain-streaked windows, and the clang and thud of constellations falling inside my broken head, percussing with the nightshift road digger's jackhammer. The mad parade of cyclists, lightbulb rainbows under bridge arches, blues songs blowing on the wind. A naked woman in the bus station on Marnix, piss running down her legs. The night heron, as ever, watching over the fisherman. Cab driver half talking, half singing along to Moroccan songs on the radio; a gang of street kids throwing shuriken ninja stars, spinning nunchuks, and choreographing kicks; the drunken dancer in the rain outside the closing café. The cab moves slowly through narrow streets, with me imagining Bernard Herrmann's *Taxi Driver* soundtrack bouncing off the houses. The mad, tilting architecture, falling into water. An imaginary city in the hallucinatory night. We get back to the squat – the very building we'll be living in for the next year – and as Becks goes to the 24-hour shop to buy the traditional milk and bread, it occurs to me not for the first time that if it wasn't for Becks, I would probably be dead. *I'm a roaming stranger, I'm a roaming stranger.*

A few days later I wake up in a hospital in Liverpool on an intravenous drip, having immunoglobulin infused into my veins. Apart from a vision of myself sprawled on a bench on a North Sea ferry, I have no memory of the journey home. And now that I am home, all I want to do is get away. So for six months I work in my dad's junk shop on Stanley Road, patching up old furniture, selling sewing machines to merchant sailors, standing on the market in the rain selling tins of paint, trying to get through the Guillain-Barré flashbacks, drinking too much. And then, when it feels like Liverpool doesn't want us anymore, Becks and I pack our rucksacks and get the bus to Paris. It should be spring but it's still late winter – once again we're travelling in the wrong season. Once again, it's about to go wrong.

The Magic Lantern

A metro ventilator grill close to the Place de la Republique is the warmest place in Paris if you've caught hypothermia sleeping in a tent in the Bois de Boulogne in winter. This is where we wait, Becks and I, for the Magic Bus to Amsterdam. The abandoned plan had been to go to Marseille and from there head for Blaines and pick up summer jobs in bars or touting for nightclubs on the promenade. We slept rough for two weeks near the banks of the Seine, just outside Suresnes. I'd read somewhere that Lucia Joyce had been incarcerated in a mental hospital in Suresnes and I became a bit obsessed with the idea that I should pay homage to her tortured soul. My main memories of my time in Suresnes are of staring at buildings that might be psychiatric hospitals and gathering sweet chestnuts in the park. We had a tent but it was useless so we slept beneath the stars, although we couldn't see the stars. The ground was so cold I woke up one morning and couldn't move, shivering, my bones as frozen as the ground. Becks boiled up milk on the camping stove, dipped chunks of bread in the hot milk. I shoved the mush into my mouth to try and get some warmth into my body. Bread and hot milk, the death's-door meal for people without health insurance. We'd never get to Marseille in this state. And so we decided to go to Amsterdam, where we knew people who might be able to help us. But the Magic Bus was late. We had already waited half a day, half asleep on the vent in overcoats, drinking cheap bourbon from the bottle. Once again, the romance of travel.

★

In Amsterdam we walk along Marnixstraat, at four in the morning. There is someone howling like a dog in the undergrowth – it seems that every time I walk through Amsterdam in the middle of the night there's someone in the bushes, howling like a dog. We sleep in the doorway of the squat on Van Hogendorpstraat, waiting for the daylight. Here we are then, once again, the next beginning, the moment before everything that follows. We don't know what we're doing here, we don't know what we're doing with our lives. But when Wim – or Bill – the Wolf discovers us sleeping in his doorway as he takes out the trash, he invites us in for coffee and we desperately accept the invitation. This is what we hoped for, a shelter in a broken dream. A moment to think, to work out what to do next. He does our thinking for us. We've only been here a few minutes when he says, 'Of course, you must come and live with me!' He shows us through to his bedroom. 'This is now your home.' Bill moves his few possessions into the corridor between our new home and the kitchen. He makes a bed from cushions and beanbags, a nest. We stash our rucksacks in the corner and lie down to sleep on a mattress on the floor. I ache all over and my gums are bleeding. The hollows of my eyes feel thin as tissue paper when I run my fingers over my skin. We sleep.

In Bill the Wolf's kitchen you could see his dreams. An insomniac, he dreamed while he was awake, the place was possessed – or agitated – with his sleeplessness. Bill's dreams were in the glower. To sit in Bill's kitchen was like living in a magic lantern, a dirty projector of his tormented imagination. It could be frightening but it could also be beautiful. And Bill could be frightening and beautiful too. Bill the haunted alchemist. You had the feeling, sitting there, that something was being *gestated* or conjured from the shadows. Sometimes, whatever it was, whatever it was going to be, was sinister; more often there was a feeling of dark but beautiful magic and the expectation that it – the magic – would happen one night, when the time was right. It might take years, or forever. We sit in shadows and wait, watching him stoop over his stove, an alchemist, a demented saint. A loose strand of magenta hair falls into the skillet, becomes part of the marinade. Delightedly, he croons his favourite phrase, *Not to believe!* He speaks other strange, murmured monologues, like private songs, *Catholic shadows... old man knotted hands... the German in the churchyard... Not to believe! I have my dog... I fell today, yes it's true, a man can fall, it's not a problem... I paint my hair, the girls will laugh with delight... I would never go home before midnight, the Germans were so cruel... In Rotterdam I was the Queen, and the boats came in...* Bill was engaged in a much greater project than cooking meat, stooped over his stove, knife in hand, tiny, ignited lights dancing around him as more stray, lacquered hairs fall into the flame and float off into the shadows like angels. Sometimes he glances up, as if he's spotted a version of himself projected onto the walls, a younger Bill, his own legend. He laughs, *Not to believe!* He murmurs about deaths and loves, aches and pains, betrayals. In its darkness, its enchanted gloom, its glints of fire, its aromatic mystery, we are inside his hallucination. The room is his imagination. Becks and I sit for hours watching the magic lantern show, and hear about the young Bill, who danced all night, who kissed the boys and kissed the men, who drifted through the dockyards of Rotterdam writing strange poems of men in boats on oceans. He fell in love. He fell in love again. He made sure that he always had a broken heart.

One of Becks's many skills is shoplifting. I never saw anyone else pilfer with such ease, such casual grace. Robert Bresson would have adored her. On our first morning living in Amsterdam, we go to Kalverstraat so that Becks can steal toiletries from the HEMA. After she's lifted toothpaste, soap and candles she goes out into the street and steals a bike. It doesn't occur to me at the time, but we're already parasites. We speak in broken vocabularies. A kind of secret code. Side-of-the-mouth English, snatches of bad

Dutch. We don't want anyone to know that we are who we are, we want to fade into the background. We don't want to be English. If anybody asks, we tell them we're from Ireland. Our itinerant identities are provisional, evasive. We walk the streets, beginning to recognise other itinerants. We are the people who don't quite live here yet, who might be going elsewhere.

We collect empty beer bottles in the streets and take them to the night shop where we exchange them for cash and buy flip-top Grolsch. We sit in Bill's kitchen, slugging from the bottles, watching him tend to his marinades and skillets, as if we are all waiting for him to come back home from the strange place in his head, seeing how his years in a prison camp in the war have made him live in nightmares. *My body is burning. Their instruments are inside me. I am falling into oblivion. I am 16 years of age. My parents are invisible. I am an orphan. I have no tomorrow. Not to believe. I misdirect Germans. They ask for the museum, I send them to the recycling. I have scattered flowers at memorials. All the pretty boys are ashes. My body is an experiment. When it ends, I wander empty streets, and everyone is dead.*

We become Bill's family. I help him peel mushrooms, marinade meat, stir his concoctions on the stove. He is cadaverous like Herbert Huncke, glamorous like Quentin Crisp, flamboyant, gin-soaked, a carnival in stack-heels, all chiffon scarfs with a brooch at the throat and daubs of lurid rouge. A sacred monster who'd had one novel published a long time ago, a story of dockside cafés and brothels, loosely autobiographical, a Jacques Brel song come to life. He disrupts every street he walks down, spectral, disturbing the crowd through sheer hauntological presence – and he is heroic. Rouged, henna-haired, like the couture priestess Marcheta Casati, shoes click-clacking on the cobbles. Bill is madly in love with Harry, a much younger heroin addict who lives downstairs in an abandoned electrical shop. He cleans Harry's needles and wounds with lemon juice, and sometimes, when Harry is cold and lost in narcotic withdrawal, Bill takes him into his bed and holds him tight. Harry is a big hearted, gentle soul with a Roger McGuinn mop of dirty hair and a grin that would light up his face if his teeth hadn't fallen out long ago. He wears the same psychedelic woollen jumper every day and sleeps in it too, rolled up to reveal the track marks, scabs and sores on his arms. Sometimes, we hear Bill singing softly to sooth Harry to sleep – Bill, Harry and the Alsatian dog all huddled up in a heap of rugs and blankets. I scribble their stories in my notebooks, try and get the colour of their characters down, trying to learn to write about these people, and finally start to feel I'm living in the sort of underground paperback I loved. I even tell people I'm a writer, but am still in thrall to the Beats and pay more attention to the costume than the syntax. I am a complete novice – a novice at writing and a novice at living

The house has its own weather. A shabby supernatural aura. It feels like it's sinking into the city with the weight of its own melancholy. Everything feels damp, oozing, defeated. Black tongues of wet mould hang down the stair walls, emitting phlegmy liquid. Makeshift pipes drip warm, oily fluid that doesn't seem to be water. Four floors high, anonymous, polite, you wouldn't know it was a *kraken-huis*, a squat. Even Harry the heroin addict on the ground floor, and the dealer living in the loft, are discreet in their day-to-day activities.

On the first-floor lives Nina, a Portuguese artist who paints everything pink including her clothes. Her ceilings are festooned with upside down paper parasols out of which pink paper roses spill. Pink hair, pink lipstick, pink nails. She has a Josie and the Pussycats tattoo on the bony wrist of her smoking hand. Mondo the dealer is a heavy brooder, and never speaks to anyone. A malevolent presence who inveigled his way into the house by grooming the woman who is now his girlfriend, an English nurse called Mandy, who has been addicted to morphine ever since she fell in love with him. The trapdoor to their loft is padlocked and probably booby trapped. It's all a bit Johnny Thunders up there – paranoid atmospheres, clandestine activity. Their toilet is a bucket. We often see them leaving the house, carrying the bucket to slop out at some designated spot down by the dirt boat, the floating skip where Amsterdam dumps its old kettles, two bar heaters and toasters. Sometimes they just open the skylight and throw the slop on the roof. From their window, down to the yard, there is a Heath Robinson-esque walkway built from planks and guttering for their cat to climb up and down. The tabby likes to sit in the yard, sizing up Harry's pet rabbit in its cage. And meanwhile, in Bill's kitchen, camped out on a sun-lounger, is Robicheau. Jean Gerard Armando Robicheau, the Belgian mercenary, rumoured to be on the run from the military police. Robicheau is – unexpectedly given his curriculum vitae – a charming soul. A pipe smoker with faded tattoos on his arms and neck, tilted gaze, watery eyes. He, hardly speaking English or Dutch, has picked up Bill's habit of saying *Not to believe!* The buildings echoes with the phrase as the two men express their disbelief in just about *everything*. In the middle of the night, Robicheau wakes up and kills mice with his boot, dropping them in the dog's food bowl, so Arpet the German Shepherd can gobble the corpses.

Harry wakes in Bill's frail arms and reaches for a cigarette. Beyond the curtain that separates our room from Bill's corridor the two men are whispering their love for each other. I watch them through the gap in the curtains – pink curtains painted pink by Nina. You can feel yourself walking through ghosts in this house, and in the evenings, as the sun goes down, you can see them in dark corners. We don't know the history of the house, and don't need to. Perhaps we are the ghosts, or the ghosts to come.

★

Becks and I have settled into Bill's old bedroom. We sleep on a mattress on the floor. Sometimes a mouse will climb up the rattan window blinds above our pillows and disappear into a crack above the pelmet. We eat pasta and strange yoghurts sprinkled with chocolate chips. We eat paprika crisps because we have never seen or tasted them before. Most of all we drink vast quantities of Grolsch (the cheapest of Dutch beers in those days). Our family of strangers sit in fading sunlight – Bill, Harry, Jean, Nina, Becks and me. The house takes on the character of Bill's darker moods. The house *is* Bill. Becks gives him a present of stolen ruby nail polish. He paints his nicotine-stained nails, trembling fingers, pausing to suck on cigarette or spliff, murmuring his mythology. In the smoke of weed and cigarettes, in the murmur of our voices, one voice emerges as the central presence as Bill's memories unfurl in smoke.

The boy grew up in Rotterdam, born in the 1920s. He knew he was different early on, felt more like a girl than a boy, liked dressing up in his mother's clothes, clattering down the street in high heels. He liked boys. By the time he was in his teens he was on the corners, flirting, kissing boys, kissing men. He ran away from home, went underground, ran with a gang of outlaws, thieves, anarchists, poets, rent boys. Fairground hauntings, dockyard loitering, pinball cafés, market halls, cheap hotels, dance halls and pissoirs, motorcycle pillions with bee-stung lips and pouting in railway stations, lusting after dirty sailors. Life is a cabaret. Life is a carnival. Life is a brothel. Life is a prison cell.

Bill's story changes every night. When war breaks out, he is a vagrant, an undesirable, vermin. Sometimes he is taken in by a holy man who prays to God to save his soul. Sometimes he is picked up by the cops for distributing anti-Nazi pamphlets on the streets. He ends up in a prison camp, still in his teens, flamboyantly queer. He tells us that they tortured him, burned his body. He tells us things until he can't tell us anymore, and starts to cry. He falls into the broken sleep of insomniacs.

In the night, a mouse climbs up the rattan blinds. And then there are two mice. And soon there are three, four, ten, more. We fill in holes in skirting boards with newspaper. The mice claw and nibble at the newspaper and the noise keeps us awake. 'It's just a few mice,' says Bill. 'After all, this is Amsterdam! Like in the song.' We buy mouse traps and poison from the hardware store. In the night, the clack and snap, the silence after. We are all insomniacs now.

Pale Colours, Shimmering

I write letters home to my parents, to my sisters Val and Kathryn. My mum and dad write back to me, care of Poste Restante. Twice a week I go to the Central Post Office and pick up my mail. I cycle along canal streets on my stolen bicycle, thinking, *Not to believe.*

I don't believe my memories. I am suspicious of the way they fall – or slide – into my thoughts and glow in half-erased pale colours, shimmering. I wonder if I've invented them or borrowed them from someone else and wonder why these capsules of ephemeral oddity keep coming back to me, especially when I'm homesick or nostalgic for dreamlike yesterdays. When we went to see the dead whale on the back of a haulage lorry, and I watched the men with hose pipes, spraying the corpse with water. When we saw Billy Smart standing at the entrance to the Big Top, smoking a fat cigar. When we saw the conger eel at the Pier Head, and I was frightened again. When we went to the Dancing Waters in T. J. Hughes at Christmas, and it wasn't very good. When we had our photograph taken with the monkey. When I got sunburned on the beach at Prestatyn and my dad carried me back to the caravan. When the stag jumped across the bonnet of the car on a quiet road in Scotland, but Kathryn missed it because she was on the floor drawing with crayons. When Uncle Ron locked us in the meat freezer in his butchers' shop for a laugh and Val and I thought we were trapped and would die but Dad released us. When we drove slowly across the Yorkshire moors and stared in wonder at Fylingdales early warning system, the alien spheres glowing in drizzle and mist. When Dad made us a skateboard in work but broke it while he was showing us how to do it and got upset. When Dixie the dog nearly drowned on the frozen boating lake but Dad kept us calm and rescued him. When we saw moths bigger than our hands. When I saw a girl sunbathing on a deckchair and thought that pretty girls smelled of tomatoes but the smell was coming from the next door neighbour's greenhouse. When we saw the nuclear power station and the dead gull at exactly the same moment. When the inflatable dinghy capsized and Dad pulled me out of the water. When Dad took me to Uncle Les's cobblers' shop and Les showed us how he kept nails in his mouth. When my shoe fell off my foot on the Mersey ferry and we watched it float away down the river while I cried. When Dad gave us money for hot chocolate from the swimming baths vending machine. When we tried churros on holiday in Devon and he bought another bag straight away (we licked sugar off our fingers). When I fell in the river in the Trough of Bowland and was embarrassed and angry and Mum and Dad hung my clothes to dry on a fence and wrapped me in a picnic blanket to keep me warm. The Prudential man's fingerless gloves. Elsie Barmaid's back-alley trysts. When Mum was in hospital having a hysterectomy and Dad cooked Sunday tea (we didn't like the gravy). When we broke open the earth and found fossils inside and held them in our trembling hands. When my sister Val was dying in 2019 and he went to see her every day, walking from the train station – even though he was in pain with arthritis – because your children aren't supposed to die before you.

I don't think of the past as being somewhere *back there*, somewhere in history. I think of the past as being *right here, right now*. The past is in the present, perhaps tentatively adjacent, *just there*, tangible, within reach. I don't understand when people say, *You're dwelling in the past* as if 'The Past' is elsewhere, somewhere negative, unworthy of attention, a place we should stop visiting.

How can the past be thought of as an abstract place you visit in your head when it's a place that is *here now*. In the same breathing space as the present? Hallucination interwoven with material reality. And what about nostalgia? Nostalgia is a tainted, problematic idea, something we are encouraged to be ashamed of. Something that is holding us back, stopping us progressing, going forward? What if we translate nostalgia into an enhancement, a seasoning ingredient? What if it were possible to be 'future-facing' *and* nostalgic? Sitting here and now in Liverpool, thinking about Amsterdam in the 1980s, I don't feel as though I'm living in the past. I feel as if that life I lived is still being lived *now*, is here in this room, in the shadow and light of the present. And I'm trying to think about memory more and more – or even more than ever – trying to work out why it feels like *a place*.

Vital spirit, that early morning breeze, the genius loci, the sense that there is more to bricks and concrete than just their physical materials. That there is another dimension that alters and imbues the city with meaning. I tend to think of shadows – *the shadowplay* – as the space of memory, but it's also there as an essence in the breeze and the spaces in between. The pneuma of the past and present, coming together *in this moment*. Perhaps that is memory: the city remembering the forgotten.

The Wingspan of the Heron

I go in search of Bill's the Wolf's novel, but I don't know what I'm looking for. He has never managed to describe what the book is, or even what it's called. *I wrote about the waterfront... the boys! I wrote about... amusements, the fading... It doesn't matter... Nothing matters... I wrote it in the voice of my youth but now I am old... My truth is broken,* his voice drifting off into the shadows, into the walls of the house. I search for hours in libraries and old bookstores. I ask the assistant in the bookshop on Spui but he has never heard of it. He looks through catalogues, there is no mention of Bill or of his book. I search through boxes of rain-damaged hardbacks in the flea market on Noordermarkt and the tarpaulin junkheaps on Waterlooplein. No sign. We sit together in a café on the square. *Once I rode on motorcycles,* he murmurs, *life was such a joy! One day I will tell you about the places... the prison camp, the sanatorium, the whorehouse.* He laughs, a smoker's rattle, watery eyed and gentle. Flecks of ash in his magenta hair. *One day, you must read my book.*

I get a job on the nightshift in the Sonesta Hotel, which fancies itself as being a cut above. Mister Boom the supervisor reminds me of Ashby, my Geography teacher at school, an absolute sadist. The foreman's name is Muhammed Ali, and he runs our team like the chain gang in *Cool Hand Luke*. We are English, French, Irish, Moroccan and all of us are illegals. There is an implicit code of signals, eye contact, nods. We keep our heads down. Even though there are machines to do the job, he makes me wash pots and pans. Hours drag by, hands in greasy water, scrubbing congealed fat off filthy skillets. Even though cleaning is *actually my job* I'm outraged at being told to do it. The night before a council inspection we have to clean the kitchens from ceiling to floor, otherwise it would never pass. Eight hours on my back, scrubbing the undersides of cooker hoods and ducts with aluminium cleaner and scouring pads, soap and grease falling in my eyes and mouth, clothes dripping wet, snaking my body down the metal guttering, elbows and shoulder blades in spillage. And crying, crying with sheer tedium and pain, while Muhammed Ali pokes at my feet with a spatula and Mister Boom, feet up on the desk in his office, spoons herring and kroketten into his mouth. The nights go on forever, mind numbing tedium. One night I sneak upstairs to the lobby and watch hotel guests returning from a night on the town. A couple who fancy themselves as Burton and Taylor, sweeping in from their taxi, click-clack of shiny shoes on polished tiles. They have no idea that the kitchens in the bowels are filthy, that the cooking pots are hand-washed by people like me who scrape the congealed fat off with disgust, that the place is only cleaned when an inspection is due, that there are mice and cockroaches everywhere. I duck into the hotel resident's toilets in the lobby, curl up in a cubicle and sleep for an hour. When I go back down to the kitchen, no one has even noticed I've been gone. Soon we start taking it in turns to go for a sleep in the toilets for an hour. We make sure that the cubicles are spotlessly clean, the cleanest place of all in the Sonesta Hotel.

One coffee break we sit huddled in the loading bay, the *plongeurs* and pan scrapers, the rat-trap setters and floor-sweepers, always muttering, on the verge of revolt. But we all need the money. They've got us where they want us, on our backs, scrubbing cooker hoods. And at 7am every morning, Muhammed Ali makes us patrol the streets around the hotel, picking up cigarette butts from the gaps between the cobbles. A French kid called Marcel spits, 'Fuck this!', and gets sacked on the spot. I pick up fag butts, wondering how the hell I got here but at least it's better than the hell-heat of the kitchens. Amsterdam in the morning air, coffee on the breeze, gulls. A moment. And then, as I'm picking up butts on Singel, a man carrying a trawler net onto the Haarlemmerstraat bridge walks slowly toward a flock of pigeons eating scraps of bread. He throws the net over the birds and in slow motion, in heavy hobnailed boots, he walks over the net, trampling, crushing the pigeons beneath his feet, twenty birds crushed to death in minutes. He scoops up the net full of broken birds, tosses them into the canal and walks away, net slung over his shoulder. Early morning commuters, the man in the coffee shop doorway, the tattooist on the corner, all of us watching the nightmare, watching the bird killer turn a corner and disappear. We watch each other instead, all witnesses to an event that ought to be impossible. And then the street returns to normal, as if it didn't happen. Pale sunlight, first cigarette, cats on the Poezenboot stretching in the sun. Did it happen? If you'd walked across the bridge five minutes later, you would never know. Shaken, on edge, I decide to place the cigarette butts back between the cobbles where I found them – an hour spent placing them precisely, gleefully, a small act of disobedience, ash-ends facing like burned out curses in the direction of Mister Boom's office. A Hex on the Sonesta Hotel.

The wingspan of the heron, the fisherman's companion, is as wide as the parking space it occupies. An overcoated spectre. A heron on Herengracht! I wander through the city in the morning light, nocturnal apparitions fading into the recesses of the city to remain there until the dark returns. Bums, lost hitchhikers, drunks, addicts, dealers, casino workers, barmen, strippers, prostitutes, nightshift workers, insomniacs. The sudden realisation that these are the sort of people I live with! It's a nighttime city in many ways, and the nights are beautiful, but this is my favourite time of Amsterdam day. Spring. Pale light and the slow wander home. The city smelling of coffee roasting, brewery yeast. First sighting: the first crocuses of the year. The city has that glow, the crocus glow beneath the pale, enormous sky. Penknife out, I cut the string on the morning newspaper bundle outside a yet-to-open shop on Leidsestraat and steal *The New York Times*. In Vondel Park, on grassy banks by the lake, there are people waking, emerging from damp sleeping bags in twists of circling morning mist. Aftermath latecomers to the faded hippy dream, fifteen years too late to ride the Marrakesh Express. I recognise the willful precarity, unwashed underwear, punk-hippy shabby chic, carefully curated vagrancy. They probably write poetry. These people are me.

Down on the waterfront, through derelict wharves and warehouses, anarchist alphabets stencilled on loading hatches, cormorants deep diving. Squatter murals, bedsheet banner slogans. Territory of Dogtroep theatre company, the drained dock slowly filling up with North Sea water, musicians floating away in tidal flood. One day all this will be gentrified, real estate, but now it's a pirate village. The last days of the Graansilo, soon to become derelict, soon after to become a squatted citadel. Territory and last hurrah of the kraaker movement. An unauthorised peoples' free state of civil disobedience. Unlike the shy and retiring squat I live in, these buildings are in your face, provocative, up for a fight, wild and revolutionary. A flyer on a telegraph pole saying YOU JUST WANT TO TOUCH MY BODY, with a photograph of cops beating a protestor with night sticks. I peel the flyer from the pole, fold it into my pocket to later pin on the bedroom wall.

The *kraakhuisen* are such beautiful provocations. Outsider art, statements of dissidence and intent. Painted slogans like manifestoes, Situationist blasts on bedsheets, establishment-baiting cartoons, more stencilled quotes from anarchist bibles. The squats we visit mostly house English skivers, French and Swiss petty criminals hiding out from arrest warrants, dopeheads, remand absconders, scavengers, veteran anarchists, Zen Anarchists, bullshit anarchists. At a party in a warehouse on Oude Schans, not far from Rembrandt's house, we meet Martine the Parisian matriarch of the house, an heiress who *messed things up a little* and was cast out of the family, losing her inheritance. Travelling in Tunisia she contracted a life-threatening disease, and she says she doesn't expect to live for many more years. She has a moustache, never bathes, laughs like a lioness and steals towels from the hotels she works in as a chambermaid. *One day I will bathe, and I will use all the towels.* Her lover, Clive, is a weed-head, some kind of petty criminal who can't go home to Chelmsford ever again. He is always *moving on,* but he never goes anywhere. It never happens and probably never will. We are all living in the never happens and probably never will zone. Our lives are itinerant and so are our desires. Our only ambition is to find something of value in the streets or the dirt boat that we can sell to buy more weed. From the dirt boat, Martine has gathered out-of-date supermarket food, dumped, now turned into a salvage-feast for the party. Gouda fondue bubbling hot in a pan as big as a cauldron. Bruised fruit salad, butterscotch Angel Delight, broken children's Disney birthday cake, rough Cabernet squeezed from the polyethylene bladders of flood damaged box wines. Ghetto blaster, full blast, Henry Cow's *Amygdala* and Zappa's *Uncle Meat* on rotation. An English misfit dressed like a Druid sings story-songs, like a mystical Jake Thackray who's slipped too many Mandrax. Three mallet-wielding Mohawked drummers stripped to the waist hammer out oil barrel Burundi. There are jugglers and a contortionist. It's like Tom Waits's *Swordfishtrombones.* Clive huddles over a trestle table making 'Indian Games' out of beads and twisted wire. Everywhere you go in Amsterdam there are English deadbeats selling these games – three days after buying one they fall to pieces in your hands. A man who calls himself 'The Sheriff' sells us a bit of weed. He works in live sex shows and lives in a windowless basement room, a solitary confinement cell, where he writes anarcho-manifestos which he distributes on Dam Square. Twenty years in the future I will see him again, on Bold Street, Liverpool, selling Indian games. This gathering in an abandoned warehouse is the feast of the lost souls' subculture, of the misfits who have found each other, the avoiders. I am one of these people, willfully irresponsible, drifting without purpose or ambition.

Outside in the street, road workers start digging up the cobbles at three in the morning. 'There's gonna be a raid,' says Clive, and everyone at the party who hasn't got residents' papers scarpers, leaving only the Dutch and legals. Parked up on the corners, police vans wait for the signal to move in, arrest, evict. Cycling home through the Red-Light District, my front wheel falls off and I go headfirst over the handlebars. Sprawled in a heap in the ultraviolet glow of a hooker's window, I realise someone has sabotaged the bike, tampered with the wheel. In the coming weeks, everyone we know who lives in a squat starts getting edgy, more paranoid. It all adds to the excitement of living in between the city's cracks.

A shabby-chic underground aesthetic prevails. Stokely Carmichael, Eldridge Cleaver photographs ripped from magazines, Symbionese Liberation Army cobra stencils, Patti Hearst is a terrorist pin-up. Weathermen revolutionary texts, Baader-Meinhof fascination, sweetheart crushes on Astrid Proll and Che Guavara. We've all read and half-digested Edward Abbey's *The Monkey Wrench Gang*, Richard Neville's *Playpower*, Emmett Grogan's *Ringolevio*, as if by reading the paperbacks we can absorb revolutionary spirit. Emmett Grogan has read the books I'm reading: Gary Snyder, Philip Lamantia, John Weiners, Jack Spicer, Robert Creeley, Leroi Jones. A guerilla library of dissidents, dropouts, delinquents and bad influences. Martine and Clive even give me a bookshelf one day, and I cart it home through the Red Light, propped on the pedal of my bike. I begin to fill it, and find more on the steps of the Central Post Office, on my way to pick up mail from Post Restante. A carrier bag full of books: Hunter S. Thompson, Deirdre Bair's Samuel Beckett biography, *Wolf Solent* by John Cowper Powys and two pairs of fishnet stockings. On Sunday afternoons, I go to the American Discount Bookstore on Kalverstraat and sit on the floor leafing through books I don't necessarily understand and feel no need to. Grove Press editions of Beckett, Genet, Robbe-Grillet, City Lights editions of Frank O'Hara and Ferlinghetti, Patti Smith's *Babel*, Kathy Acker's chapbook, *Hello, I'm Erica Jong*, the thrill of Anna Kavan's *Julia and the Bazooka*. Four Sundays in a row I sit on the bookstore floor reading Richard Fariña's *Been Down So Long It Looks Like Up to Me*, and on the last Sunday I walk out carrying it, an unintentional theft. It's here now, on my desk, inscribed on the title page, *Jeff Young, Amsterdam, June 11th, 1983*. A paperback portal to a book thief's past.

At the end of a nightshift in the Sonesta, Mister Boom tells me I'm being transferred to the Koepelkirk to do something or other at a business conference. I haven't got a clue what he's talking about, and he doesn't care to explain. He tells me to go home, get shaved, come back in an hour wearing a clean white shirt. I suspect this is a ruse to get rid of me and I tell him I don't own a white shirt and don't much care for shaving. 'This is the Sonesta Hotel, Mister Young. We don't have three-day beards in the Sonesta.' He refers me to head office to discuss the matter and I cycle there, unshaven. Why didn't he just sack me at the end of the shift? Why go through all this? The receptionist tells me to sit in the waiting room, someone will see me when they're ready. I wait an hour, then ask when I'll be seen. 'It might take a little while longer.' I wait another hour. Eventually someone calls me into an office and Mister Boom is sitting there with three other men. I ask if this is about the three-day beard and tell them I think, if it is, it's a bit pathetic. This doesn't go down well. It turns out it's about the three-day beard, the hour I spent sleeping in the toilet cubicle, the re-positioning of the cigarette butts in between the cobbles, the meeting in the loading bay in which I attempted to incite an insurrection. 'What are you exactly?' This is the question. 'What are you, you silly English man, some kind of foolish comedian?' Which makes me laugh, and I go too far. 'I suppose I'm just… fucking lazy.' It's Mister Boom's turn to laugh. He bellows until he chokes. And then he tells me to fuck off, leave. 'This is the Sonesta Hotel, Mister Young. The finest hotel in Amsterdam. We don't employ silly boys with three-day beards.' I tell him if this was England, the unions would be down on him like a ton of bricks, which just seems to exhaust the three of them. 'This isn't England, Mister Young. This is the Netherlands, where you are not welcome.' They sit in a dumbfounded, deflated heap. Eventually, Boom waves me – curlicues of cigarette smoke – towards the door and I tell him I'm not leaving. Not leaving until they pay me all the money I'm still owed. 'You will have a very long wait,' Boom says, stricken with fatigue. I go and sit outside in reception. The receptionist smiles at me, weakly. I sit there for several hours. Occasionally, I see one of the three men peering at me through the office blinds. I try to read the papers. Eventually the receptionist takes a phone call, opens a drawer in her desk, takes out a petty cash box, counts out my unpaid wages in coins, stacks them up and slides them across her desk in my direction. I thank her. Through the blinds the men are watching. And then I scoop up the money and lash it, coins spinning through the air, hitting the window, crashing down to the floor, rolling. 'Fuck you,' I say. 'Fuck you, Mister Boom. Fuck you, Sonesta Hotel.' Exit with a swagger. I cycle home, laughing, triumphant. What a day! Back at the squat I tell Becks excitedly how magnificent the whole thing was, how I showed them a thing or two. How I won! She shakes her head, tells me I'm an idiot. And then she says, 'Oh, well, at least you got paid, eh? Please tell me you got paid.'

Unwritten Codes

Magdalena sits on the pavement, smoking robustos, peeling potatoes into the bowl of her skirt. She used to be a prostitute but now she owns the Parima Hotel, a dive of a place, down the street from the bar where Albert Camus's *The Fall* is set, squeezed between leather bars, yards away from the Zeedijk bridges swarming with heroin dealers, and the dark street where Chet Baker fell to his death. There are cockroaches everywhere in the Parima, and no one ever pays for their drinks. I've got to know Magdalena from hanging out there, drinking, filling up on cheap egg and chips. I've always liked her wildness and she seemed to take a shine to me, passing on the information, the word on the street. One night she asks me if I'm working, offers me the night porter job – check in, check out, serve a few drinks – and tells me to start tonight, be there at 1 a.m. I don't want the job. I have to take the job. I have to get there on time.

But first, I go to see The Gun Club – Jeffrey Lee Pierce is falling to his knees like a cowpunk evangelist, pounding the Paradiso stage with pudgy fists, flailing around in a seizure of ecstatic derangement, like Adrian Street, the wrestler, gone to seed. The Paradiso is packed with sulphate agitated A'dam street-punks, anarcho leathers, motorcycle boots, cockatoo quiffs. We're close enough to the stage to be speckled with Lee Pierce's sweat, to stare into his smudged mascara eyes. He's wailing, of all things, *Disco Inferno* by the Trammps, *Burn, baby, burn, Disco Inferno, Burn the Mother down, Disco Inferno...* The glorious, clumsy, cowboy-booted mess of him, bewildered, comical, vulnerable, magnificent, disintegrating. Patricia Morrison is to his left, cat's-eyes darting glances at him, driving the locomotive, onwards through the inferno. But I have to leave the ritual – it's time for work. Jeffrey Lee Pierce's howls follow me through the burning church. Reluctantly, I walk to my Parima nightshift, possessed with wayward spirits.

I turn up on time and Magdalena is there to meet me, glammed up for a night at the casino, Cohiba clamped between her teeth. Her bar manager, a French kid called Michel, is there to show me the ropes. But as soon as Magdalena has gone, Michel stretches out on a bench and goes to sleep. I can see the track marks in his scrawny arms, and he has the same kind of Johnny Ramone dirty mop of hair as Harry. I stand behind the bar, clueless, wondering what the hell I'm doing here, just me and a wasted junkie on the nod. I pour myself a beer, try to calm down, try to think. I decide that waking Michel might be more problematic than leaving him asleep. I decide to improvise.

The Parima is a dirt-cheap dive with a 24-hour bar, open to the public. Given that the place is on one of the Red-Light District's sleaziest streets, the quality of 'the public' leaves a lot to be desired. The first person to come in looks like he's been caught in a storm but I check and it's not even raining. He wants a beer and a toastie and he sits on a barstool, squeezing out his clothes, watching me closely. I can manage the beer but the toastie machine is beyond me. 'There's a man over there, asleep', he tells me, helpfully. We both look at Michel with distaste – me, pretending I hadn't noticed. I tell him it's that kind of place, part of the attraction, and he seems to accept this like a recommendation. I dig a fork into the toastie machine to try and extract my customer's ruined toastie and the machine goes off like an incendiary device. Smoke and sparks, the soaking man laughing his head off, thoroughly enjoying himself. I go into the galley, looking for a fire extinguisher or blanket and – bear in mind that I've eaten here on numerous occasions – I'm physically repulsed by what I find. Every surface is covered in congealed fat. The frying pans are filthy. There are cockroaches crawling everywhere, rat traps primed and ready for the kill. The place is a breeding lab for eradicated diseases. When I go back to the bar, the soaking man is hanging his wet clothes on the radiators.

At 3 a.m. thirty Greeks from Athens come in through the door and crowd around the bar. I start pouring beers. They drink the beers. They want more beers. It seems the Rolling Stones have just played a stadium gig in Rotterdam and their Athens fans have decided to come to Amsterdam because 'the Red-Light District is better'. Feeling as if the Stones were the support act and I'm the headliner, all I can think of doing is turning the music up loud. Suddenly, there are thirty Greek Rolling Stones fans dancing to *The Best of ABBA*.

Warmoesstraat is a wide gutter, a throat in the body of the city. The oldest street in Amsterdam, a cruisers' alley of dark rooms and fetish dives, coffee shops and corner dealers. It reeks of weed and latex, espresso and mayonnaise. It has a dirty charisma. Lusty insomnia. Feral. The Parima is the unofficial home of cheap-eaters and black economy drifters. It's where the information is, and I just nearly burned it to the ground with a fork. I go outside for a smoke.

Directly opposite the hotel there's a tea merchants, a fragrant, genteel civilised presence in what Bill the Wolf fondly refers to as 'The Devil's Arsehole'. Sometimes, Becks and me go there to buy packets of loose-leaf Lapsang Souchong or Apple Spice. The shop smells of woodsmoke, pine resin, citrus petals and cherries; the people who work there are elegant and gentle, in complete contrast to the Tom of Finland leather boys in the dungeon bar next door, which smells of sweat and poppers. The tea shop is a decompression chamber, a respite from the madness.

Standing in the Parima doorway, probably trying to control a panic attack, I see Herman Brood the Rockstar – capital R – swaggering along, motorcycle boot buckles glinting in the streetlights. I often used to see him on the streets, unmistakable with that crow-black hood of hair and stooped-hustler, rolling gait. Tonight, he's wearing biker leather and zoot trousers, with girl-watcher shades in the night. Sometimes I follow him, fascinated by his deadbeat glamour, white suit, raven hair, skull rings like knuckle-dusters, tattoos that might as well say *Louche* and *Dissolute*. Tonight though, I watch him fade into the mid-watches and shadows, heading to some insomniac assignation in noir and neon.

My nerves are on the outside of my skin, not just tonight, always. I am permanently alert to dangers, which most of the time are imaginary. So much is unspoken. I live in intonation and atmosphere. As if I've achieved the invisibility and *lostness* I've been looking for, and don't know what to do there. I live in the space between two languages, in the untranslated. Apart from the Irish itinerants – many of whom are escaping from The Troubles – I hardly know anyone who shares the same language. We get by on speaking in gestures and shrugs, and sentences that sound glued together like punk blackmail lettering. Mongrel Language. This is the language of the undercity we live in, this shadow city, this phantom plane, this secret drift of the disappeared and invisible, this off the record, outlaw, *Gastarbeiter*, subterrain – this is where I am living in all its shabby poverty and glory. The Irish chambermaids, chain-smoking in lunchtime bars after the shift; the pickpockets and shoplifters; the acoustic guitar slingers and fair dodgers; the addicts and the scavengers, drunkards and deadbeats, hustlers and kitchen porters, street cleaners and bartenders, sex show workers and booksellers, the philosopher and the poet. The instinctive insistence on the awkward, the playful, the improvised and disobedient, the drift. This is where we are living. The digressive, speculative, fluctuating, wandering, provisional. There is nothing to tie my life in Liverpool and Amsterdam together other than these instinctive suspicions and refusals of the orthodox, the conventional. The shrug of indifference at the things you are supposed to do in favour of the things that you are not.

Back in the bar I serve more beers to pissed-up Athenians until they stagger out into the night to gawp at hookers lit-up by UV. The Parima is empty. Michel sleeps on. I fill a half-litre glass with drip-tray slops and pray for the dawn.

Five in the morning now, just when the end of this hell is glimpsable, the doors open and five middle-aged English men come in, sit on the barstools and order beers. They're builders from the Midlands, working on a conference centre in the suburbs. I try and conceal my Liverpool accent, but they quickly work out where I'm from and find this hilarious. 'Fookin' Scouser, what the fook you doin' here, Scouse?' I can already sense this is going to end badly so I just humour them, serve them drinks, tab the slate up on a beermat, listen to their jokes, pretend they're an absolute scream, for two hours. It's daylight outside and they want breakfast but of course I've incinerated the toastie machine, so they want chips. Michel looks like he's dead. I go into the galley, fire up the chip pan, empty a bag of frozen fries into the fat, and go back into the bar just as they're walking out the door. They haven't paid the tab. I try and wake Michel, shaking him until he rolls off the bench, hitting the floor with a thud. He's furious I've woken him. I tell him a gang of builders have left without paying the tab and he shrugs, 'Who cares? A couple of beers.' I tell him it's more like twenty-five beers and he goes white in the face. 'She'll fuckin' kill me!' he says. Never mind him, she'll definitely kill me. I run out into the street, Michel staggers after me. The gang are heading towards Zeedijk, laughing.

Banter. I catch up with them, Michel lurking, lagging behind. The gang leader turns around, nods to me, smiling. 'Y'alright, Scouse?' I'm clearly not alright. 'You have to pay the tab,' I say. 'You owe us quite a lot. Thing is, if you don't pay up I'll get the sack.' He nearly collapses laughing, wipes his eyes, doubles up at the comedy of our lives. And then he straightens up, takes me by the throat, rams me against a wall, my head crashing into the bricks, his mates thoroughly enjoying themselves. 'Don't you be worrying, Scouse! It's only a few bob. Everything's going to be tickety-boo.' And then he releases me, wipes his hands on his jeans. 'If I think on, I'll pop back,' he says, and then they walk on, like a walking tour group enjoying the sites in the early morning light. I turn to Michel, in tears, shaking with panic. 'I'm definitely getting the sack,' he says. 'Because of you, you stupid fuckin' Scouser.' We walk back to the Parima. I'm definitely getting the sack. Please God, I pray I get the sack. The soaking man is still there, tending to his laundry. 'Oh man,' he says, almost with admiration, 'That was the funniest thing! You are so getting the sack!'

Once, I had a naïve dream that travelling was an adventure, a broadening of the mind pursuit, a gentlemanly saunter, an expansion of the inner space. According to Seneca, travel and change of place impart new vigour to the mind. According to Hilaire Belloc, we travel for fulfilment. According to Anatole France, wandering re-establishes the original harmony which once existed between man and the universe. According to Joseph Roth, *I am on my own, but I have a certain sense that my destiny has me on a leash.* That's more like it! My wretched attempts at 'travel' led me here, and by 'here' I really mean 'nowhere'. This isn't even travelling, it's the avoidance of travel, nothing more than a dislocation. Everything is provisional. It occurs to me that perhaps Warmoestraat is where I'm meant to be. Destiny Street, Dead End Street, Desolation Row. It's daybreak, time to go home to bed.

★

When I get back to the squat, Becks is sitting bolt upright on the mattress. She whispers, 'Listen.' In the cavity walls there is movement, rustling, scratching, scurrying. Becks has been awake all night, watching platoons of mice crossing the room from corner to fireplace and back again, climbing up the rattan blinds, excavating the newspaper and quick-dry we have plugged the holes with. I lie down, exhausted on the mattress as a mouse runs through the gap between my neck and the pillow, brushing against my skin. Things are escalating, rapidly. Bill says it's not a problem. *This is Amsterdam after all!* I go to the hardware store and buy more mousetraps, heavy-metal weaponry, fit for the war to come. But when I get home, I can't face setting the traps. My vegetarian, *All Creatures Great and Small* instincts take over and I *pretend* to set the traps instead. No one will ever know, and the mice will voluntarily surrender and move out of the house when the weather warms up. It's going to be fine.

One afternoon when we come out of the Stedelijk after our regular visit to Ed Kienholz's installation, *The Beanery*, bicycle thieves have stolen our stolen bikes. It's part of the unwritten code of bike thieves that you just shrug, move on and look for another bike to steal. But it's now a thing we have to *deal with*, to find more *guerilla solutions* to our precarious existence. We live in this place of unwritten codes. The zone of itinerant duck and dive. We think of ourselves as being honest, but we are thieves. We tell ourselves that we only 'liberate' unlocked bikes – *we never break the locks*; this is our red line and we wear it like a badge of honesty. Sometimes we do make new bicycles out of salvaged parts – a frame fished out of a canal, a saddle found on the dirt boat, which is always a source of useful salvage. Kettles, heaters, toasters – we collect them all but can't make use of any of these things because we don't have electricity. We stockpile them anyway, storing them in the front of Harry's gaff – the part of the house that used to be the electrical goods shop. The VanHogendoorp squat is off-grid.

It has no electrical power, and we enjoy the absurdity of storing electrical goods in an electrical shop where there is no electricity. Even though the swag belongs to us now – a sort of bottom drawer for when we get our own place – Harry sometimes sells the goods to the scrap man for a handful of guilders, then spends the cash on heroin. *Keep the money moving.* It's a black economy channel where salvaged goods become hard cash, become the means of buying low-grade smack from a street dealer. An underground economy of scavenger, to addict, to retailer. Supply and demand. Without even really thinking about it, the lemons I pick up from the gutter on the fruit and veg market will end up cleaning hypodermic needles and the wounds on Harry's arms.

On most Sunday nights we go out *trashing.* We walk the streets, rooting through heaps of unwanted furniture, and so the tradition of hoarding continues, from father to son, Blitz firewood sold door-to-door becomes Staadsleidenbuurt boxes and bags of books and clothes, pots and pans, cutlery and toys. The churn and heave of A'dam recycling night. The three pairs of boots I own were found on the street. The Turkish carpet Bill uses as a bed throw was found in a bag of stolen hotel towels. The nighttime drift of gleaners, flea market dealers, scavengers, drug addicts and hoarders move slowly through the streets, turning the heaps over, digging into the crates, carting away scrap metal, utility furniture, microwave ovens, handbags. A three-piece suite on three men's backs, stooped like upholstered turtles heading for the river. It's a moving wave of the unwanted and 'might be useful' disappearing into squats and lockups, pored over by antique spivs, broken up for copper. Apart from quiet words of recognition and tip-offs about niche interests, no one ever speaks. We are the silent gleaners. There's something of the post-apocalyptic about all this, as if the underground dwellers have emerged when the city is asleep, scavenger creatures picking over the ruins.

★

One Sunday night we find a portable record player and a stack of blues long-players. Gold dust. John Lee Hooker, Sleepy John Estes, Blind Lemon Jefferson, the Howlin' Wolf. Thirty vintage blues records just lying in the dirt beneath a tree. I strap them to the bike rack on top of the record player and take them home. When Harry jacks the record player up to an industrial battery, the old electrical supply gaff is transformed into a shebeen and we dance to trash night blues.

On market streets at the end of day we forage for our supper. Fruits I've never seen in England, vegetables from distant lands. Ugli fruit, mooli, mango, celeriac, jackfruit. We pick up battered aubergine, zucchini, shallots and cook 'approximate ratatouille' on the camping Gaz stove. We raid the food dump barge near Martine's warehouse, for more Gouda cheese and tinned peaches. We take carrier bags of beer bottles from Harry's backyard labyrinth of glass to the Dirk Van den Broek Night Shop, cash them in for vouchers with which we buy more beer. And when the nights are warm, we climb up onto the rooftops and cook, and drink, and smoke, up there in rooftop land beneath the glimmer, like drunk and stoned astronomers.

One of Becks's guiding principles in life is to never pay for public transport. Everywhere we ever go she refuses to buy a ticket. In Paris, she would insist on jumping the gates or hurtling through the automatic exit gates as passengers walked through. Then she'd stand there, waving me towards her, daring me – almost threatening me – to do it. To break through the portal. Anxiety through the roof, I either try and fail to bunk the gate or end up paying, much to Becks's disgust. Sometimes in Amsterdam, instead of biking, we bunk the tram with an eye out for inspectors. If we find a *strippenkart* in the street, Becks dings it in the ticket machine on boarding just to look as if the journey is legit. It cripples me with anxiety. We always stand at the back, which is a kind of caboose or viewing area where we can spot the inspectors waiting at the tram stops. They have a disconcerting system of all boarding at once through different doors and pouncing on the scammers. On us. As soon as they hit the tram Becks side-mouths, *'RUN!'* and we're off towards the exit, shouldering past strap-hangers and ticket cops, praying that we'll make it to the street where we can dodge down an alleyway, away into the city. Nine times out of ten I get caught. Becks finds this deeply embarrassing. I have failed her. If you get caught, they escort you to head office where you have to pay a twenty-guilder penalty. If you haven't got the money, anything can happen. I'm an alien, technically illegal. My two options when I get nicked are to either run, or play the naïve tourist who doesn't understand the very complicated system. I practise this at home, try out the dialogue: *I'm on holiday here. First time. I thought there'd be a ticket man.* One time, I get chased down Prinsengracht and when the ticket cop catches me in the queue for the Ann Frank Huis, it turns out I've been to his birthday party where I gifted him a stolen cheese plant. Instead of nicking me, he gives me a gratis *strippenkart* and invites me to a barbeque.

The ruins of Gregory Corso sit propped up in a bar at the rat's end of Zeedijk – a bar with a curtained-off corner where prostitutes can take their drunken clients. Tobacco and smoking paraphernalia spill out of the pockets of his leather waistcoat, and he has two pairs of glasses hanging around his neck on lengths of string and bootlace. He had been beautiful once but now he is nowhere near holding it together. His teeth seem to move around in his mouth. His hair is like a mop of dirty worms. He's drinking what looks like cough mixture, but if it is cough mixture it's not working because he's hacking like a dog. This is the man who stole Jack Kerouac's girlfriend, and now he looks like a man who steals shoes off sleeping beggars. He is derelict. Apart from his eyes. I can see his mind working inside his head as he watches the mad parade

of Zeedijk. He's still in there, inside his own ruin. To me, Gregory
Corso is a kind of shaman, a holy barbarian, a direct link to the
counterculture, to subversion, to cultures of dissent. I stand in
the doorway of the bar and watch his flickering eyes. Just watch.
Yards from here in a few years' time, Gregory's friend Chet Baker
will fall to his death from the window of Hotel Prins Hendrik.
Whenever I visit Amsterdam and walk past Chet's memorial,
my Corso encounter and Baker's death are conflated – Gregory
is watching a prophetic vision of Baker tumbling to his death,
suspended in eternity, falling forever, never hitting the ground.
Gregory is suspending time-future, stopping his friend dying, a
magic ritual defying time and death. I pluck up the courage to go
and speak to him, tell him I love his poems and I'm a big fan of
the Beats. He is sick of the Beats, particularly the ones out West
telling farmers how to plant potatoes. He tells me we are living in a
Jean Genet novel, but what did Genet know? Corso once painted
murals on the walls of a house in Paris and upset the landlord.
The man was a friend of Genet, who came around to the house
and gave Corso a good telling off. To which Corso declared with a
sneer, 'Genet is so fucking bourgeois.' I ask him for his autograph,
and he reluctantly scrawls on the back of a postcard.

To Jess, Hi, Gregory Corso –

I tell him my name is Jeff, not Jess, and he scratches two cursive Fs
over the S's. And that is it. He sits there playing with sugar sachets
and spoons and staring at the street. And after a few minutes I
leave him to it and head to the Parima to collect my wages. On
the way down to Zeedijk, I look back to the café and see the
decaying Beat poet scuttling off into an alley. I walk down a street
full of heroin dealers, and the smell of weed mingling with Dim-
Sum is so powerful, my head so full of my encounter with Corso,
that it doesn't matter when I get to work that Magdalena fires
me. Michel is behind the bar, performatively operating the toastie

machine. He pretends he's never met me. Looking at me with pity, Magdalena shakes her head. I ask for my wages. She laughs and says, if anything I owe *her* money.

Slow walk home. *Face the music. Can't face the music.* Robicheau is standing on the Marnixstraat lift-bridge, smoking his pipe, on his way for a morning cognac. He gestures, do I want to join him? We go to a bar. Line up the drinks. The day heads slowly into oblivion. We do not speak. We look at his tattoos, blurred smudges, inky military slogans. His secret injuries are hidden inside him. Whatever his past is, his skin doesn't want me to know the stories. The tattoos are erasing themselves. Unwriting secret codes.

Collected Lightnings

The room is lit with candles, and resting next to our pillows there are torches. Beyond the curtain in the corridor, Bill is sleeping quietly with Harry in his arms. Robicheau is sleeping on his bed of sofa cushions on the kitchen floor. Arpet the dog is somewhere, waiting for the plague. We can hear the mice in the wall cavities, and they sound more like one writhing body, shifting and *fawumphing* in the claustrophobic darkness, determined to escape. Beast of Dark Cavities, Lord of Claustrophobia. Waiting for the moment, dramatic effect its ultimate priority... We lie in wait, and periodically a scout will come out of hiding, usually a baby, swaggering on the diagonal across the room, glancing up at the wardrobe inside of which a raiding party scuttles around the Tupperware boxes where we store our snacks. Prankster mice taunt us from the rattan blinds. The loose cannon that likes to sneak between my neck and pillow is just sitting, staring at me, perhaps *laughing*. We switch the torches on, dazzle them, they retreat. It's like a rodent Colditz. And then it happens – the staples fixing plywood sheets to wooden frames start popping, one by one, like the teeth in a breaking zip. The walls *rupture,* and out through the gaping maw comes a tidal wave of rodents, spilling out and over each other, countless hoards of the fuckers, this way and that way, across the floor, over the mattress, a flood-tide infestation. I am standing in mice. Becks is on the window ledge swearing her head off. Beyond the curtain Bill is wailing, 'I believe you! You were right! The house is full of mice!' In the kitchen, Arpet is howling and eating the ones that Robicheau has clubbed to death with a souvenir wooden clog. And Harry is fast asleep in the pillow nest, in the almost-death of opioid dreamland. All night we fight invading forces. They keep coming in waves. In the morning we collapse exhausted into our makeshift beds. The dead, dying and wounded are everywhere. Many survivors have disappeared into a hole beneath the shower unit. Others have slipped into the shadows, under the door, out onto the landing. *Clip clippety clop on the stair...*

One night we go to a bar near the Dam to hear Gregory Corso reading. He sits, cross-legged on the stage, still wearing his leather waistcoat, one pair of glasses tucked into his rats-tail hair, the other pair hanging around his neck on a length of string. He reads like a man with no teeth, a gummy, lisping drawl. The poems are chewed on like tobacco, his streetwise delivery at odds with the formal style of the verse. It's tender and sad and vulnerable and it doesn't feel like we're in the presence of a rebel poet – more like we're listening to a kindly old neighbour who's been through a bit of a rough time. After the gig the Bard of Salford, John Cooper Clarke, is drinking with Corso at the bar. While Becks chats to JCC about Liverpool and Eric's days, I watch Corso fiddling with his glasses, looking like a tired man who just wants to go home. The last I see of him he's pissing against a wall down a back street, Gregory Corso caught short on his way home.

When you live in Amsterdam on what they call 'The Black', you are living by the skin of your teeth. You go to certain bars because that's where the information is. The Knowledge. Someone always knows where there might be a job, someone has always heard a rumour about a place to live. No one has an ambition other than to make enough money to stay a bit longer. No one knows why they want to stay a bit longer, but they're not quite ready to move onto the next place, where they will find the bars, where the information is and do the same thing all over again. We are fugitives from something, choosing to do nothing. No one wants to be in the place they came from but one day they will go back there, *when the time is right.* Until then we are the drifters, the fugitives, the skivers, the deadbeats. Some of us have secrets – like Robicheau who *can probably* speak English and Dutch but chooses not to. If people knew he could speak those languages he would be compelled to tell his story, and then he would be even more diminished as a man than he is now. He lives in such a state of camouflage that if he were forced to communicate it would blow his cover. He is armoured against vulnerability. Most of us live in a state of lost-soul innocence, but Robicheau knows exactly what he is doing. The rest of us, we haven't got a clue. So, you drift, you fall into things, you improvise. You drink in The Three Musketeers or the Last Water Hole. You pick up a tip on a cleaning job and a place to live for nothing or next to nothing and you get by. You sit for hours in a bar on Warmoestraat where the Irish chambermaids drink after their shifts cleaning the Kabul, and you cadge roll-ups and Heineken and shoot the breeze about road trips you'll probably never go on. You fall in love for no longer than an afternoon with a sweet girl from Kilkenny, and you watch the street together because the street is where the dirty glory and wonder of Amsterdam is at its height of madness. You romanticise it, you are a romantic, you are never going home again but of course you *do* go home, walking slowly through the labyrinth, just as it gets dark.

And in the summer you go to Vondelpark on Sunday and listen to the bands for nothing. The Honeymoon Killers; Paolo Passionato & the Pennies from Heaven; The Ex. Six bottles of Grolsch and a bag of grass, sitting there on the grandstand eating fries with mayonnaise. You get a two-guilder haircut and a hash cake in the pop-up hippy market, and you take an afternoon nap, lakeside, your head resting on your lover's belly. You buy a scratched copy of David Bowie's *Pin Ups* from a kid who found it on the dirt boat, and you fall in love, for a fleeting moment, with a woman cooling her feet in cool lake water as she sings to rainbow diamonds in the sunlit fountain.

Sometimes you go to the flea market and buy secondhand clothes. You buy an Eastern European military shirt because you want to look like Neal Cassady on the cover of *The First Third*. Like most people you know, you wear a battered German motorcycle jacket until the day you have an argument on Herengracht and your girlfriend throws it in the canal. In the winter you wear the woollen overcoat – the one with the dogtooth fleck – and the one-size too small paratrooper boots and the Palestinian keffiyeh that everyone in Amsterdam wears in solidarity until the day you stop wearing it because it's inappropriate to appropriate. On Thursday nights you walk the length of Kalverstraat and Nieuwendijk, weaving through the sonic montage of music blasting from ghetto blasters balanced on the shoulders of kids in from the housing projects, the dissonance parade. At least once a week you walk *very slowly* through the huddle of Hells Angels, sprawling in their armchairs outside the tattoo parlour they use as their headquarters; you know that you're trespassing on their turf, so you keep your eyes fixed straight ahead and enjoy the edgy nervousness you feel, and you like the weary boredom they show at your tiresome, pointless disruption of their code.

You go to the Melkweg where you drink Rum Tea and eat hash cakes and you watch Jonas Mekas and Jack Smith films flickering on the walls. One night you watch Nico singing, funereal and sick, her skin like grey parchment hanging on her beautiful bones, her mournful voice echoing through the bodies of the faithful. The junkie Priestess moaning, eyes closed, *Janitor of Lunacy, Paralyse my infancy, Petrify the empty cradle, bring hope to them and me...* There doesn't seem to be any hope among the hopeless acolytes, those wanting to be damned.

★

There's always someone haunting a coffee shop doorway, always someone wearing a Bob Marley T-shirt and a Rastafarian tam, always someone scraping the foam off a Heineken with a spatula, always an enormous dog tied to the leg of a barstool in a scattering of sawdust. There's always a sleight-of-hand magician doing tricks with a pack of playing cards, always a mime artist shadow-walking a tourist, always a dealer hissing *hash, spid, cocaine,* always a chess player at a card table smoothing out the baize. There's always a pipe-smoking antique seller loading up his bike cart with a bedstead, always the smell of roasting coffee and the tang of vinegar coming from the herring man, always the clang of the tram-bell coming around the curving track and the tinny bike bell ding of the bicycle rider, basket full of flowers, always the barrel organ man shaking his coin tin, always the violinist playing Vivaldi in the echoing arcade.

You become obsessed with TT Fingers, the street musician. Squatting on his fisherman's stool beneath a paper parasol, amped up acoustic flat on his lap, porkpie hat pulled down on his brow, the man is like a blues buddha, moaning out, 'Bright Lights, Big City', Jimmy Reed's steady rolling warning song, *'Bright light, big city, gone to my baby's head.* Chain-smoker croak, street-hustle stoop, broken hearted soul. Some days you walk the city streets looking for him, spirit lifted when you hear his voice coming down an alley, from Dam Square. Rent party singer cast out in the daylight with an archivist's knowledge of the urban blues vernacular. One day you see a pimp slot a fifty in his breast pocket, TT keeps on singing as the pimp steps back and bows with respect. The crowd gathers around, sensing they're in the presence of something, someone strange and other worldly, someone in a psychic space that no one else can enter. He's a lightning conductor, a soul shaker. The fingers of his left hand are missing. A metal slab, duct-taped to the stump of his hand, sliding along the strings, emitting a noise that sounds like voices, like ghosts. He's frightening. You watch him for as long as you can handle it and then you walk on, his voice following you through the labyrinth.

You watch a beautiful creature they call The Walking Sculpture sashaying down the cobbles, plumes of taffeta and plastic streamers trailing behind him in his slow-motion wake. Fabiola, aka Peter Alexander van Linden, teetering on impossibly high platform boots, fascinator millinery tilted over painted brows. A vision, a harlequin bride, a visitor from a distant galaxy. There is a glimpse of him in Ed van der Elksen's film, *A Photographer Films Amsterdam*, his portrait of the people of the streets. He moves through the frame, a science fiction apparition, altering the city as he travels through it, a catalytic, kinetic art form. Barbarella meets Jobriath. An event. When you live in Amsterdam on The Black, you are always moving into the decisive moment – as if into the photographer's framing of an ephemeral event, a moment that will last forever in the mind's eye. You turn a corner, you don't know what's going to be there. If you don't turn that corner you will miss the point where everything changes for a moment or forever. And that is where you live.

When Harry goes into rehab after OD'ing on low-grade street Methadone, he gives us the keys to the old electrical shop on condition we adopt his dog, Dullobodozo (Dullo for short), a lanky Bouvier with mongrel interventions. Harry says that the fairytale character Dullobodozo is the Dutch version of Rumpelstiltskin, but I've never found any evidence of this. He's a dog with a strong attraction to water, which in Amsterdam is somewhat problematic. Whenever we take Dullo for a walk, he slips his leash and jumps in a canal. I fall in love with him. I even love him when his fur falls out and red metallic fleas crawl over his red raw skin. Children in the street point at him, laughing. He's an embarrassment. He sleeps on the bed, scratching. It's not actually a bed, more a platform built from tea chests with stuffed coffee sacks in lieu of a mattress.

Living in a former electrical shop is like living in a Bruno Schulz story. The Brothers Quay could animate our lives: naked dog puppet, tin can flea puppets, broken doll humans in catacombs of dust motes and lightbulbs. There are dead fluorescent light tubes stacked up against the walls like a conceptual art installation, a broken Flavin & Judd. The broken tubes emit a powdery dust, like talcum powder. When a rare ray of sunlight manages to penetrate the gloom, it illuminates powder puff dust like morning mist.

The kitchen is an old lean-to extension, and the cooker is our camping Gaz, one burner stove. We become experts at balancing four cooking pots in a tower, rotating the pots to either cook the contents or keep them warm. Macaroni is eaten most days, because it's cheap. Scavenged vegetables, seasoning from sachets nicked from snack bars. When the food is cooked and hot, we nip over the road to the automat and buy two cones of fries. A feast.

The bathroom – or rather the toilet room – has no floor, just a heap of builders' rubble and a toilet with no seat and no flush. I improvise a floor out of an old tabletop, wedged, tilting, on top of the heap of half-bricks. To flush, you have to fill a bucket at the kitchen tap and pour it into the toilet bowl with force. There is a fridge in the shop front but because there is no power, we use it as a storage cupboard to protect food from the mice – there are fewer mice down here but there's one rather endearing fellow who ambles through the place in the evenings and studies us with great curiosity. On trash night we find a box of office carpet tiles and Robicheau fits them in the 'living room', cutting them to size with a switchblade. We buy a hundred candles a week and the place flickers and glows like a magical grotto, smelling of hot wax and marijuana. There is a woodburner that Harry has cannibalised from an oil drum.

One night we throw a 'New Home' party and Bill serenades us with obscene shanties. *Oh, the drag queens and the whores they slapped each other's arses raw...* Like Jacques Brel's Grandad, lit by burning furniture. Asthmatic, overcome by fumes I have to retreat to the backyard. I sit in the heart of the beer-bottle labyrinth and Bill comes out to nurse me. He holds my hand, gently. *We are here, two poets... we can weep, or we can roar... Not to believe... the dogs are dancing... tender is the mongrel, wild is the wolf... I am the wolf, Bill the Wolf, I hold your hand to sooth you... hush goes the lullaby, my lover is in the unit where they will heal his wounds...* He is beautiful. Ragged, decaying, broken. His cheeks are rouged like ripe plums and his lips are cherry red as children's sweets.

It starts to rain. The sky is dirty purple, and in a flash, it opens up with violent streaks of lightning, raindrops fall, the size of old English pennies, falling onto the glass labyrinth, beer bottles pinging like xylophones. Bill conducts the orchestra of weather, summons up the lightning, the tympani boom of thunderclap. Bill the Lightning Conductor! Bringer of Storms! Queen of Van Hogendorp in the night on fire.

When I was a boy, I saw a flying saucer. At that point in my life, it was the most beautiful thing I had ever seen, hovering over the garden in the flashing lights of an electrical storm. I assumed this alien spacecraft was charging its battery, hooked up by cables to lightning streaks. It swayed over the rooftops of neighbours' houses, as if on Gerry Anderson, Animatronic strings. After watching it for a while I suddenly became frightened, and ran to the kitchen where my Mum was cooking the evening meal. *Come and look at this!* She came with me to the living room window and stood with me, watching it, the pair of us awestruck at the sight of this spinning visitation from a distant star. And then, as a fork of lightning struck the chimney pots of Mrs Symes's house, the saucer suddenly shot up into the thundercloud and disappeared. Even as we watched it, I wondered if I'd imagined it, that it didn't really exist. But I *convinced* myself *and my mother* that it was there, in the sky, strange news from a faraway galaxy. It is possible to imagine visions so vividly that you make them come true. Many years later, when I mentioned it to my mother, she said she remembered seeing it so vividly that it was like a photograph of my imagination. I had projected the picture in my mind onto the thundercloud, like a lightning ignited conduit of dreams.

On the rooftop of the building in the early morning light I am shaving Bill the Wolf. His magenta hair is held back off his face with a chiffon bandana and his chin is tilted as far back as he can manage because of his osteoporosis. There are tears in his eyes – he says it's influenza. 'For the best of all possibilities,' he rasps, 'it makes sense if you write under an assumed name. I will take your stories to the editor and my name will be on the manuscript, no? It makes absolute sense but of course... Once I sheltered in doorways of old warehouses... I touched the mouths of mariners... I fell into the arms of dangerous men and I became a wolf just like my name. I will tell you stories and you will write them down because you haven't lived and there are no stories in your soul... Not to believe... Stories of anarchists and opium, stories of animals... We have lost the animals we used to be, forgotten our wild souls. Once I held a dead man in my arms on a train full of soldiers. Once I fell in love.'

I was beginning to realise Bill couldn't remember anything with certainty. His parents were dead, his parents were alive. He couldn't remember meeting his parents, he loved them, he was an orphan. He had been in a concentration camp where he was tortured, he had escaped to England at the beginning of the war, he had never been to England. He once had a wife and he loved her deeply, he had never even kissed a woman, he had a son that he had never met, he met his son when he was seventeen. He could never love a man, he fell in love so easily with men and knew when he was five that he was queer. He had written the great novel, the Rotterdam *Ulysses*, he had only written one potboiler book, and no one ever read it. He was writing a book now and it was going well, he couldn't find the muse and he would never write a word again. It didn't matter. Now, I was going to write his book, his name would be in the newspapers! I would have the knowledge that I had written the words, but it was *his* book. *Not to believe...* The razor blade nicks his lip, and he licks the drop of blood. 'My blood, it tastes of Jenever!' When he falls asleep, I look closely at his rouged cheeks and the pale powder on his closed eyelids. I wash the razor in the enamel bowl and climb down through the skylight. It is time to walk the labyrinth.

The house is brooding, damp, almost malarial. Haunted by the haunted. Even in the summer it is dark. Musty stench of cigarettes and salvaged carpets, rodent shit. Mondo, the dark presence, the heavy cloud, always up there, brooding, only occasionally glimpsed on the stairway, slouching out on his way to a pick up or drop off. So malevolent that even Harry wouldn't buy his gear off him, choosing instead to pick up in the park. You'd hear the trapdoor swinging open, lowering, and then the thud of his footsteps on the stairs. If you coincided, he'd brush past you, turn away, his girlfriend Mandy pulling the trapdoor up like a drawbridge, sliding closed the padlocks. Because of Mondo nobody can breathe.

Micro-destructions – I came across the phrase somewhere. This is what was happening, often self-willed. There were no major disasters. Nobody – yet – was killed. Turbulence and unease could only lead to some kind of disintegration. I began to decipher

Robicheau's tattoos, the blurred messages sinking into his skin. They spoke of guilt and sin, of death. Self-inflicted daubs of fear and loathing. *A Heart of Darkness* inked into his chest. Bill the Wolf retreated into himself, into his troubled sleep, wrapped around his dog, grieving for Harry. He hardly ever spoke, moped about in carpet slippers and a rug shawl, chain-smoking.

Becks and I are invited on a winter's night to a dinner party to celebrate Robicheau's fiftieth birthday. Or sixtieth. He tells us a different age every time we ask. The host for the night is a man called Rinus who lives in a flat he is constantly renovating from scavenged materials. Consequently, there are no floorboards and instead of glass in the windows there are stapled polythene sheets. The dinner table is balanced on floor beams, and to move around the flat we have to tightrope walk along the beams, precariously, drunk. Rinus has the look of Kirk Douglas if he was addicted to methylated spirits; swollen capillaries, exploded nose, eyes that are permanently red and swollen. He just missed out on being good looking and instead he looks like death on legs. Rinus doesn't like us, and we don't like him, but we're all here for Robicheau and we will do our best to rub along.

There's a lace tablecloth on the dinner table, a candelabra, serviettes. A plastic bin full of homebrew. The centre piece is an uncooked ham-shank and there doesn't seem to be any urgency to cook it. The urgency is all about the drinking. Bucket-brew, barley wine, Night Train Express, Thunderbird – all the ugly drinks, the brutal booze. As usual we have no common language – smatterings of Dutch, bastardised French, and the only time Rinus speaks English it's usually an insult. He chews his contempt over in his mouth like a man struggling to masticate a rancid chunk of meat. He spits, 'You fuckers, you fucking locusts!' He roars with laughter, fist beating the table. Robicheau sits, smokes, mumbling a story about Angola, something really dubious about the Congo. The atmosphere is... *negative*. Pinned to the ceiling there's a Batik-printed sheet illustrating a primitive galaxy. Beneath this dimly-lit Solar System, we are broken planets and moons. Candles flicker, spliff and cigarette ends glow. The gas stove burns but nothing is being cooked. And Rinus spits, looking at me, 'Gastarbeiter! Motherfucker Turkish man!' I ask him what's wrong with the Turks and he spews out a mangled conspiracy theory about a secret invasion, through the back door, a great replacement strategy to take over the Netherlands, and Becks and I are part of that invasion. He stands up, raging, pulls a knife, lunges at me. And I think for the first time in my life I let fly a fist, right between his eyes. He stumbles backwards, falls through the floor beams, straddles a beam, screaming, *Gasterbeiter! Parasite!* He struggles to his feet, full on pugilist fisticuffs, posturing that makes me howl with laughter. And then I'm on him, the pair of us in a flailing heap. He starts pulling my hair out in handfuls, me, shouting, 'Leave my fucking hair!' Becks is on him, kicking him in the ribs. And suddenly, Robicheau is turning over the dinner table and throwing bottles out of the window into the street, singing *Happy birthday to me... Happy birthday to me*. He's holding the ham shank, like a ceremonial orb. And then he hurls it, out into the street where it falls in silence. I get up, leaving Rinus flailing, and I go to the window. Snow is falling, the pavements are covered in a light dusting of white. Rinus stands, scoops a mug of homebrew out of the bucket and downs it in one. Becks and I leave. In the street, in the snow unbroken, there are four bottles of barley wine. And in the centre of this still life the uncooked ham shank, lit by a sudden, glorious streak of lightning.

Nightshift

On a cleaning job at the Amro Bank HQ in Amstelveen, I
met Big Tony, an American ex-soldier who had married an
Amsterdammer and narrowly avoided serving in Vietnam. A giant
of a man with a flask of sugary iced tea permanently swinging
in his hand. Easygoing. A shadow-boxing soul who liked a drink
and *Just wanted to get by, no hassle.* Big Tony was going home to
Washington DC to visit family and needed someone to cover his
nightshift in a bakery café on Kalverstraat. Four weeks work. Cash.
I turned up at the place at 11 p.m., and Big Tony showed me the
ropes. As we worked he told me about his life, about the difficulties
of being an African American in the military, of falling in love with
Ellie, getting married, getting out of the army, and getting out of
being sent to Vietnam. He was so in love with Ellie it didn't matter
that he couldn't get a proper job in Holland. He was happy doing
cleaning jobs on what he called *the slow and easies*. He wasn't here
to work, he was here to be in love. The job was an easy but tedious
eight-hour shift of cleaning, restocking the shelves, polishing the
floors and windows, and taking out the bins. As well as bread and
pastries, baked on the premises, the café sold Belgian chocolates
and Big Tony had a sweet tooth – it's amazing how many chocolates
you can fit in your mouth in one go. There was a rhythm to the
job – Task/Rest/Eat/Drink/Repeat – and it was easy to get the
hang of. In the morning, as daylight creeped onto Kalverstraat, Big
Tony took me to one side as we were cleaning the front windows.
'Listen,' he said. 'It's important that you steal. Steal as much as
you can. Anything. Everything. Just steal it. Because, if you don't

steal shit, they'll know I've been stealing shit for seventeen years.' I nodded, said I'd do everything I could to do the job properly, and then he gave me a big bearhug and strolled off into the city to get ready for his holiday in Washington DC.

At home, I tell Becks I have to steal. I'm sick of stealing but Becks says I have to think of Big Tony. If I don't steal, I'll be letting my friend down. So, theft is now a duty of friendship. On my first shift, I let myself into the café and stand there, looking at the shelves. I follow Big Tony's example and as I work through the routine, I drag a binbag around with me, dropping a pack of honey waffles into the bag, a carton of Belgian chocolates, a couple of pecan pastries. It doesn't exactly feel like criminality, not like robbing a bank vault. It's a bit pathetic. So, I decide to up my game. In the cellar, I liberate an Edam cheese and a bottle of Chateauneuf Du Pape. 1kg of Douwe Egberts goes into the binbag. Lapsang Souchong, why the hell not! Twelve small bottles of Paderborner pils. Butter, milk, ham, sugar, two loaves, some more Belgian chocolates. Just before 1 a.m. I take a carton of raspberry ripple out of the fridge, tie up the bin bag, carry it out into the back alley and pass the goods to Becks who stashes it into her bike basket and pannier bags and cycles away, loaded down with swag.

Towards the end of the shift, I can hear the bakers arriving and chatting, baking away, singing along to the radio through a wooden hatch in the wall. I have never been introduced to these men, and I will never meet them. As the nights go by, I begin to enjoy the proximity and the mystery, not knowing who these men are. They are characters in a Samuel Beckett radio play or ghosts trapped in the walls. They operate in a separate world, as if their manifestation of the city occupies an overlapping, palimpsest space to my manifestation of the city. We are in the same building, but we are invisible to each other. I work in silence – don't want to draw attention to myself. Perhaps they don't even know I'm here.

I clean customer toilets – each night there are sprays of dried blood on cubicle walls, the blood of heroin addicts who come here to shoot up. While tourists sit downstairs in the café, eating apple cake, there are junkies sitting on toilets with hypodermic needles in their veins. I squeeze the cleaning rag into the toilet bowl, water turning pink, junk-blood flushed away into the sewers. A sticker on the toilet door says *I HEART AMSTERDAM.*

At 3 a.m., while I'm polishing the floors, an apparition appears at the front window, at first as a finger drawing in condensation, then becoming a shadow-presence, then becoming a man, peering into the café, watching me. This happens nearly every night in the month I work there, and it takes me a while to recognise him. I step back into a dark corner of the café. It's the man from the Eben Haezer all those years ago, the man with the cardboard sign hanging around his neck, the levitating demon. The Thief of Souls.

Whosoever Looks at Me Invades
My Body and Steals My Soul

I feel sick. I don't know what to do. He beckons me. I retreat. Beyond the hatch, the bakers have fallen silent. What if he's one of the bakers? I dismiss this idea and opt for the ominous: what if he's been waiting all these years, searching for me, finally finding me, the nightshift thief? Kalverstraat in the early hours is usually shutters down, damp and oppressive. The only sound you can hear is the pub singer belting out Johnny Jordaan tunes in the bar that never closes. The nightly insomniacs walking the streets are mostly passing through their own ruminations and anxieties, pondering some unreachable mystery. Most of the time they are unaware I'm in here, watching them, or more likely they don't care. But the demon knows I'm here. I am the reason he's wandering the streets in the desperate hours. He beckons me. I walk slowly towards him and just as I get close to the window he disappears. This keeps happening, and on the nights he doesn't visit me, I miss him. I want him to be with me in the night. He is my only companion.

One night a car pulls up outside with a yacht towed behind it on a trailer. The driver takes out a set of keys and lets himself into the café, hand in hand with a woman dressed in silk. He introduces himself as the owners' son and asks me to make them a coffee. He never introduces me to the woman, who he can't stop touching. They sit on high stools at the counter and drink their coffees slowly. I clean and restock shelves; he watches me but pretends he isn't interested. I convince myself he's here to investigate the mysterious disappearance of large quantities of cheese and Belgian chocolates. He strokes the woman's thigh, whispers in her ear, glances in my direction as if to say, *Look at me, a guy with a beautiful woman... and look at you, some loser guy with nothing...* I nod. *I have stolen your Chateuneuf and I don't give a fuck.* They go downstairs for twenty minutes and I hear laughter. When they come back, straightening their clothes, I am supposed to be thinking, *What a guy! Oh, I would give anything to be in your yachting shoes...* He gathers up his bunch of keys and leaves, taking his woman by the hand, popping a finger-gun at me. Everything is property – the woman, the car, the yacht, the stupidity. His car won't start.

The malevolent shape of the thief of souls is here again, draped in blankets, magical totems and cardboard placard hanging around his neck on a beaded necklace, *Whosoever...* I go out into the street intending to confront him, sick of his antics, his mad kabuki psychic war. I should hit him. I want to hit him. If I can hit Rinus like I did that night at the dinner party, I can hit this idiot. He bows to me, hands pressed together as if in prayer and salutation. And then he does that mime artist slow hand down the face thing, changing his expression from smile to sadness. I start to laugh, dismiss him with a wave of the hand, turn to walk away, and when I glance back over my shoulder he's disappeared. I have exorcised the demon. He no longer exists.

At 5 a.m. every morning I go outside to clean the windows. I like this time of the nightshift most, the light coming up and the day-city starting to awake, taking over from the night-city gloom. Hosing down the windows, watching the soapy water flow across the pavement and into the drain, I feel an unfamiliar sense of contentment. I don't know what to do with this feeling. Of course, it doesn't last. But before it fades away, there is the highlight of the shift – the daily appearance of the rollerblading man, bringer of joy, wearing nothing but a metal studded leather thong. Every morning he comes twisting and turning down Kalverstraat, nods to me, pirouettes, speeds away – an 'only-in-Amsterdam' event.

I decide I'm not awake, this is a dream. A dream of workers, sleepwalkers, insomniacs, lost souls, thieves, roller-blading fetishists, addicts, ghosts drifting through the nightshift realm. The dream is manifesting the drifters, perhaps to tell me a story. Perhaps the story is that I am one of the lost souls, insomniacs, sleepwalkers. One of the ghosts. Each morning, when I get home, the thief's feast is laid out before me. Becks has arranged the stolen goods on the kitchen table like a harvest festival. The meat, the cheese, the booze, the biscuits, the chocolates and the bread. We breakfast on pecan pastries and red wine. The drunken feast of thieves.

When Big Tony returns from Washington he resumes the nightshift, and a few days later we meet up for a beer. He hugs me, looks into my eyes with pride. 'You did good, kid. You did very good stealing.' I had done well. I *had* done good stealing. And for the first time in Amsterdam, I didn't get the sack.

Old Ladies of Willemsstraat

Contamination. Oud Bou chews her gums as she holds out her hand and mutters the word, *Besmetting!* I've read this word in *de Volkskrant,* the Dutch newspaper I try and read over morning coffee in De Vergulde Gaper café. I think the article I read was about pollution, but I think Oud Bou is implying I am the pollution. In her outstretched hand there is a goldfish – a dead goldfish, and she holds it under my nose so that I can see its deadness. I'm not sure what I'm supposed to do, so I hold out my own hand and she drops it into my palm with distaste – distaste for death, distaste for me. Mimi, the upstairs tenant who is a bit more amenable than Oud Bou shouts down from her balcony, 'She thinks you've killed her goldfish!' I tell Mimi I haven't touched her goldfish and Mimi replies, 'You have killed it by your presence. Your very being here, this is the cause of death.' I close my fingers over the corpse and, done with it, done with me, Oud Bou turns on her heel, spits a gob of tobacco juice and goes back into her apartment. I suppose the moral of this story is: don't fuck with pet goldfish that belong to retired nuns.

A week ago, Harry came out of rehab and returned to the VanHogendoorp squat. He liked what we'd done to the electrical shop, and he wanted it back. Suddenly, we were homeless. I took Dullo for one last walk to the Westerpark. As usual, he slipped his leash and jumped straight into the lake where he stood, motionless, letting the cool water sooth his bug-bitten skin. I sat on a bench watching him, watching Amsterdam. Grey heron in ragged overcoat; dealer passing a bag of weed to a tourist then scurrying away with a fist full of cash; a woman cycling slowly with a trailer full of children; the sudden weather of the city turning from sun to rain and back again in moments. When Dullo had had enough of his hydrotherapy, I pulled him out of the lake and we walked back to the squat, the dog covered in pondweed and slime. Harry was carrying bags of cement into the electrical shop to build a proper bathroom. You can't help but love him. He's clean, healthy, chubby, free from the demon. He gave me a hug and I handed him back the keys, keeping the spare set so we could sneak in and steal the fridge a few days later. I gave Dullo a hug and walked away in tears. The VanHogendoorp days were over.

And then we went to say goodbye to Bill who hugged and kissed us fondly, but quite rightly he was tired of sharing his home with house guests and mice and didn't invite us to stay. We watched as he retreated into his alchemist's laboratory, possibly forever, stirring strange concoctions in his skillet.

Luckily, by then we were on more-than-nodding terms with a man called Erik who always wore a green nylon tracksuit. Erik liked to do good deeds, so we'd often see him carrying shopping for old ladies or carrying a carpenter's toolbox to someone's boat to do some DIY. Sometimes I would go out with him, riding pillion on his illegal moped. Every time we stopped at traffic lights the engine cut out, so we had to get off and run, pushing the bike until the engine kicked in again and I had to run after it, jump back on, go wobbling off across the tram tracks, up the river to Amstelveen and the Amro HQ where we cleaned desks and vacuumed carpets for three hours, ate some canteen leftovers with Big Tony, and then rode home. I liked these rides with Erik. The freedom of the journey, moving down the riverbank and into the city, like characters in a film. I was one of Erik's good deeds. I liked that surrender to the man in the green tracksuit, to the agent of chance on a broken moped. At a houseplant party at Wall-Eyed Benny's, Becks and I get talking about our housing predicament and Benny – who resembles the *Carry On* comedian Bernard Bresslaw – calls Erik over and suggests he *give us a chance*. We don't know what this means, so Erik explains that he's shortly going travelling to Galilee, to look for Jesus, and his apartment will become available. If we want to do a trial week living in the flat, he will decide if we are eligible to take the place. The catch being, we will share the flat with a gang of Algerian outlaws – he says the word *outlaws* with affection, as if it's just another word for *family*. Not knowing for certain what we were agreeing to, we say yes, that sounds brilliant, and shake hands to seal the deal. The next morning we pack our few possessions and bits of furniture salvaged from the street, and carry it to Willemsstraat. Through a covered alley into the courtyard, we are suddenly bombarded with vegetables, kitchen utensils and the fury of old women, screaming, spitting, angry.

Erik lives in a ground floor cold water apartment with no bathroom, facing onto an almshouse courtyard garden – one of the many secret gardens in the Jordaan. The house used to be a retirement home for convent nuns, but as the nuns died off, *civilians* moved in and the only surviving nuns are Mimi and Oud Bou, Erik's grandmother. No one ever explains how she managed to be a nun *and* a grandmother, but we let that pass because things are weird enough. And these nuns and grandmothers are hurling missiles and hurling abuse. We hide beneath our furniture, holding a coffee table above our heads as we run through the bombardment. We get into the flat, lock the door. The floor is covered in mattresses. Sitting on the mattresses, backs to the walls, are the Algerians. The Gang of Three. Hakim looks like Rainer Werner Fassbinder, complete with hoodlum leather jacket, fat, chain-smoked spliff clamped between his teeth, dirty tache, army fatigues; Medusa, his wild-haired girlfriend who only ever seems to wear T-shirt and knickers, sometimes not even the knickers, has a permanent Gitane on the go, dirty black eyes dazzling, smeared in kohl, burning over the rims of children's shades; Zuthimalin, Hakim's brother, slack-mouthed, body stooping to the left as if he's had a stroke, wears a Guevara beret, and his birdlike hands dance around his mouth as he gestures with a cigarette in one hand and a lighter in the other. Zuthimalin – shortened to Zuthi – has a pet rabbit and a budgerigar in a cage, and although having pets doesn't really fit with the outlaw atmosphere around these people, Zuthi dotes on the rabbit, tickling its ears as he tucks it inside his shirt. The budgie looks unhealthy, scrabbling in the dirt on the bottom of the cage and pecking half-heartedly at the cuttlefish poking through the bars. This menagerie adds further unease to the vibe in the room. *It's weird.* The fourth person in the room is someone we know: Robicheau, sitting like a spliff factory over a scattering of weed and papers on a copy of Disraeli Gears. It seems these people are his friends. Becks is already retreating out the door with a FUCK THIS face on, but I take her by the hand and coax her across the mattresses where we prop ourselves against the sink and nod and smile nervously at our new housemates. Robicheau passes the spliff. We all relax. For now. Home Sweet Home.

When Erik comes home, we have a meeting. The plan is for a sort of competition – over the course of a week Erik will make mental notes about the way we behave, the way we treat the apartment and community of old ladies. Do we keep the place clean? Do we keep the noise down? It's hard to imagine how a criminal gang, clearly on the run, can tick any of these boxes, but at midnight we all bed down on the mattresses, and Erik – who likes to sleep in close contact with wood – folds himself into a kind of casket made from lengths of fencing and panels from old wardrobes. The Algerians take this with a pinch of salt, but Becks and I are transfixed and horrified by what we're seeing. *Is this a test?* We sleep, fitfully, the rabbit hopping over the mattresses, the budgie pecking cuttle.

I really can't sleep so leave Becks and go walking in the night. Along the river docks, the factories and warehouses decay. A railway line winds through the ruins. I walk the tracks overgrown with weeds, before 'edgelands' were invented by psychogeographers. Desolate and beautiful as a Tarkovsky landscape. *I am being watched...* I climb inside an industrial silo through a rip in its metal skin. Somewhere nearby I can hear angle grinders, eating into salvage. Scavenger alphabet, secret codes are scrawled onto the ruins. Information, territorial markings. I'm nervous in these trespass zones. Who will I encounter? Anxieties over contaminated materials, chemicals, asbestos. Suspended from a gantry there are reels of copper cable. Oil drums full of zinc, aluminium, lead. Someone's stash. A shadow moving through the rafters, through toxic water dripping down into sump. *This is someone's home...* As morning light rips the fabric of the building I sneak back out, through the watcher's shadow, out into the dawn and home to Becks, still fast asleep on our mattress, surrounded by sleeping outlaws.

Two or three times a week I go to the Staadsleidenbuurt library and read James Joyce. The library is a hideout from chaos. There's a good English language section, mostly Irish literature and between *Dubliners* and a few pages a day of *Ulysses*, I read *At Swim Two Birds* or *The Crock of Gold*. My head is full of philosophers and poets, crooked timber and drunks. *If I'm going to be a writer, this is what I must aspire to.* I sit down and begin to write a novel. Just like that, like it's normal. Notebook open, black ink drawing pen on the table. In my bag – the leather satchel I found lying on the tracks on Liverpool's dock road – there is a copy of Peterson's *Field Guide to the Birds of Britain and Europe*. I carry this totemic book everywhere for the simple, ridiculous reason that I have read somewhere it's Malcolm Lowry's favourite book and therefore it must have magical properties. Folded in my notebook there is a photograph ripped out of the NME of Captain Beefheart in the Mojave Desert. I carry this totemic photograph with me for the simple, ridiculous reason that in the song 'Ice Cream for Crow', Don Van Vliet sings magic to a crow, ...*don't shake my hand, give me your claw, two tears in a haystack, scarecrow get back, tonight there's gonna be a feather treatment, beneath the symbol we'll all assemble, oh how we'll fly, oh how we'll tremble...* I take a copy of *Ulysses* down from a shelf and I sit and think of Buck Mulligan and Captain Beefheart's crow, and this is how I believe I will write my masterpiece. And I don't write a single word.

Robicheau turns up in the library, leafing through the newspapers, and I get the feeling he's been following me, watching. He joins me. He thinks I'm stealing books. He understands my craving for pages. 'Je vous ai vu. Dans les entrepôts.' *In the warehouses, I saw you. Not to believe.* He points at my notebook. I tell him I'm writing a novel. A novel about him. He laughs, he likes this. It appeals to his vanity. 'Bad guy, eh?' He mimes an imaginary switchblade. I know he has a real switchblade in his pocket. *Not to believe...* He tells me I should join the library. The more ID I have the better – a wallet full of ID keeps the authorities off your back. Then all you need is a Giro bank account and before you know it you qualify for social security. He makes it sound so easy, so reasonable. I get the application forms. Robicheau seems proud of me, like I've graduated into an academy. I don't know what he's playing at. Again, I imagine war crimes, at odds with his keen interest in libraries. I fill in the form and take it home for Bill the Wolf to sign as a referee. Infamous author signs library application for budding genius/ghostwriter. It's all falling into place.

★

I haunt Island Bookstore. At first on Kloveniersburgwal and then when it moves to the narrow Eerste Egelantiersdwarstraat off Prinsengracht. Island specialises in Black Sparrow, City Lights, New Directions. I buy Allen Ginsberg's *TV Baby* and John Clellon Holmes's *Visitor: Jack Kerouac in Old Saybrook;* Burroughs's *Cobble Stone Gardens.* Books with a touch of DIY about them, small press waifs. I begin to write fragments of story in my notebook – observations of Nina who has changed her colour palette from pink to monochrome, building junk architectural structures in her apartment like the Dadaist Kurt Schwitters's Merz sculptures that took over his Hanover apartment. *She is breaking and entering new dimensions. She is preparing to slip the bonds of gravity.* I bump into Bill in the Westerpark and as we sit on a bench, I show him my writing. He says, 'But my dear, you need to be writing about me!'

In a secondhand English language bookstore run by an American man, I take Wyndham Lewis's *The Apes of God* to the counter, but the man won't sell it to me, explaining that Wyndham was a fascist and the book will fill my head with negative energy. I go back on three occasions, and he refuses to let me buy it. On the fourth occasion he says, 'Look, I'd rather you stole the fucking thing! Just fucking thieve it.' So, I shoplift the book while he's serving another customer, and as I'm walking down the street the same customer comes hurrying after me, puts his hand on my shoulder and says, 'I saw what you did. That book is stolen.' I try and explain, that it's *stolen with the permission of the proprietor,* but it doesn't compute, and the man starts marching me back to the bookshop. I decide to make a run for it. And so I'm legging it past the Hells Angels sitting on their sofas in the street and one of them sticks his foot out. I swerve, trip, stumble and the stolen book skitters into the doorway of the Angels HQ. I just stand there, surrendering to the absurdity, members of the Oakland Chapter watching me with interest. I try and explain: *Intended to pay for... tried four times to... the man wouldn't let me... oh what's the fucking point.* I pick up the book and offer it to the biker who tripped me up. 'I don't want the book, man,' he says to me. And then I begin to say, 'I think you'd like it. He was a fascist just like you,' but think better of finishing the sentence. Possibly a step too far. I think he's going to kill me. But instead of kicking me to death and dumping me in the canal, he laughs. They all start laughing. I stand up and walk away and the laughter follows me, as does the man who attempted to make a citizens' arrest. 'They're really nice guys, especially the Oakland Chapter,' says my new friend. He apologises for misunderstanding the book-theft situation and he walks with me to Willemsstraat, introduces himself as Max, an exile from Paris who lives on Marnixstraat, and then his killer line: 'I'm a mystic.' This is all I need. Maybe this is *exactly* what I need. I invite him in for coffee and Medusa is doing Tai Chi in her underwear. Things are beginning to escalate.

Six in the morning and Hakim and Medusa are having sex. Erik is up, brewing coffee on the gas. He doesn't seem to notice – or doesn't care – that two of his 'guests' are fucking. *Surely this disqualifies them?* Erik just smiles – not at me, at them – like a kindly hotelier enjoying seeing his guests settling in. Becks is already awake, sitting in the courtyard on a deckchair. Feral cats parade the walls, yowling. Oud Bou – Erik's grandmother, Mevrouw Jan Brouers – is suddenly there with the goldfish and the insults. I take the goldfish from her hand and go to bury it in the garden. The poor, lifeless goldfish has lost its golden sheen already and it lies on the flagstone as I dig a hole, grey as a piece of lead. Becks is already awake, sitting in the courtyard on a deckchair. Feral cats parade the walls, yowling. After I've buried the fish, we go for a walk to the end of Brouwersgracht where we sit on a bench eating chips and mayonnaise. A dredging barge is moving slowly through murky water, churning up debris, the hydraulic arm and grab clawing into the cut, pulling out heaps of mangled bicycles dripping in weed and polythene, dumping them in a heap on the barge, a trawler full of rusting metal beasts. We watch, fascinated, the ugly underbelly of the city vomiting in public. The words just spill out of my mouth, from somewhere lost inside me, words that I might have muttered to myself but never dared speak out loud: *I feel a bit... suicidal.* It's the most frightening word I've ever said. Like an ugly animal crawling from my mouth. Suicidal. Dipping chips in mayonnaise, close to tears. Suicidal. The lowest I've ever felt, sick of my own wretchedness. Even though I've said the word, I immediately know I'm not going to kill myself. I think I've said it to frighten myself. To make something happen. I suddenly feel I've gone too far, uttering the word, but Becks isn't frightened of the word. I nervously look into her eyes as she licks mayonnaise off her fingers and I can see she's already working on a plan to take the edge off the moment. Off the enormity of the word. So, I say, quietly, that sometimes I get lonely. And then suddenly I'm not lonely because of Becks. And then suddenly there is laughter, as we watch the bicycle dredger. The absurdity of the vision – like that winter day when the canals were frozen and people threw bin bags full of rubbish on the ice, insulting the Amsterdam picturesque, turning it ugly. The heat of decomposing waste in the sacks melting the frozen water. The spectator sport of watching until the ice cracks and the rubbish sinks beneath the surface. And so, we watch the bicycle dredger pulling metal skeletons out of the canal and the word suicidal fades away.

We go to a bar on Haarlemmerstraat and listen to Augustus Pablo. The melodica lifts our spirits, *East of the River Nile* like a theme tune over the opening movie scene of two drifters close to fucking things up and then not fucking things up, moving from despair to glimmer. *Look at us!* On Haarlemmerstraat, in an old bank converted into a café screening black and white films, we drink rum tea and watch Mae West in *I'm No Angel,* the warm, sugary rum taking the edge off the night and the dark and dangerous word I wish I'd never said.

★

We go back to the Willemsstraat flat where Erik is waiting for us, and the outlaws are sitting cross-legged on the mattresses like school children expecting the headmaster to give them their good behaviour awards. But it's us, we've won the prize – Erik would like Becks and me to live here. And instead of killing us, the hoodlums stand up, shake our hands, embrace us and gather up their possessions. They're so gracious and accepting that I almost don't want them to go. But off they go, Hakim shrugging into the alley, Medusa and Zuthimalin presenting us with the rabbit and the budgerigar as housewarming gifts. Erik gives me the keys, the rent book, a hug. Before he leaves, he turns and says with a beaming smile: 'One more thing! You have to look after my grandmother. If anything should happen to her, you will wish you had not lived.' He laughs, I feel sick. We wave goodbye, Becks holding the rabbit, me holding the birdcage with the dying bird pecking at the cuttlefish and scrabbling in the gravel.

Drift Archives

My new friend Max is washing my hair in the kitchen sink to rid my mind of negative energy when Oud Bou comes into the flat saying she wants to visit the goldfish grave. The grave is now more of a mass burial chamber because Zuthimalin's rabbit was killed by alley cats on our first night as custodians, and the wretched budgerigar dropped dead soon after. I walk Oud Bou to the far corner of the courtyard garden and she mutters prayers that sound more like curses, chewing the words in her gums and spitting them out in a glut of tobacco spit. We look at the soil where the bodies are buried and as I pat Oud Bou awkwardly on the shoulder, I realise she is crying. She doesn't remove her hands from the pocket of her pinafore to dry her eyes, she just lets the tears roll down her wrinkled cheeks. And I feel so tender towards her, she's so childlike in her sorrow and vulnerability that I feel a warm rush of love towards her, and I attempt to embrace her. Out of the corner of my eye I notice Mimi watching from her balcony, shaking her head, and then she shouts, 'Don't touch her! You must not even think about it!' I take a step away from Oud Bou, Mimi nods, and I tiptoe away. 'She is very fragile,' Mimi says. I imagine me embracing her as she turns to dust and blows away on the breeze. We watch her, Oud Bou, mourning her goldfish, sweet in her fragility and grief.

Max continues washing my hair. He's washing my hair because water is healing, and he is neutralising my demons. I really like him. Sometimes we go to Au Bout De Monde, Amsterdam's 'wisdom bookstore', where he pulls books off the shelves and reads them out loud. Grimoires, Zen Anarchy texts, esoteric philosophy. He tells me he's making a science fiction western – actors cast according to their star signs. It isn't really happening and it's never going to happen, but Max needs to believe in it, he needs to believe in anything and everything that makes his world stranger. I tell him about *MAXAGASM*, Sam Shepard's abandoned film for the Rolling Stones, the ultimate shamanic acid trip. 'My name is in the title. How did they know about me?' Max stops washing my hair and stands there thinking about the enormity of this. Everything connects. Max is the Marnixstraat Mystic, everything is available to him – Tarot, Astrology, Water Spirits, Ouija, the Mayan Codex, Spirituality. Because the house in Willemstraat is haunted by the ghosts of nuns it's a 'clean space' apparently, but somehow demons have managed to get into my head, which is why my life is chaos. Water is healing. Water will make everything okay.

A man sleeping in the Willemsstraat phonebox turns out to be a friend of ours from Liverpool called Burco. He tends to dress like Clint Eastwood in Spaghetti Westerns – poncho, hat, boots, an attempt at a high plain's-drifter aesthetic. He's hitched up from Paris with Simonette, who lives in a box room above a laundromat in the Red Light District. He's been looking for us for days but all he knows is the name of our street. And so, he's been sleeping in the phone box, keeping an eye out for us, and can he stay with us for a while until he gets his act together? Burco has fallen in love with Simonette, his hitchhiking companion. Even though he's only known her for a week or so, *when he gets his act together* he hopes to move in with her above the laundromat. He only knows one other person in Amsterdam and that person is a hashish smuggler who drives up from the Rif Mountains once a month with his hubcaps full of kief. The idea is to get settled in the box room with his beloved, if she'll have him, and then get cut into the Moroccan delivery system. Oh, and one more thing – Burco has toothache and needs to see a dentist. Wired on deep cavity abscess energy, Burco is a hand grenade. He stashes his rucksack and opens a flip top saying, 'I've got a really good feeling about living here with you. A great feeling.' He makes himself at home.

We've just stolen Harry's fridge and we're carrying it across the Marnixstraat lift bridge when we bump into Harry. He stops to chat amiably, and we put the fridge down and do the small talk. It's awkward. The flat is coming together. This morning we 'liberated' a bed frame from the scrap dealer's boat and Robicheau has gifted us a writing bureau he found on the street. Now that we have electricity, a fridge is on our shopping list, so the logical thing is to 'liberate' the one from Harry's that we used to use as a cupboard. We stand around the fridge and Harry uses it as a table to roll a cigarette on. He pats it like you'd pat a large puppy or a child. *Nice fridge.* We enquire after his health and he tells us he's clean, *more or less.* And then we hug, pick the fridge up again and start carting it towards Willemsstraat. He watches us go, offers to help but we politely decline. And then he shouts after us, penny dropping, 'Hey! Why are you stealing my fridge?' We don't look back.

Night heron, rag and bone in winter tree, rising and falling slightly, broken-spoked umbrella. I sit in the dark, as close to it as I can get, and together we watch the fisherman, his cold breath mingling with the smoke from his cigar. We are in a folktale. For a fleeting moment I am a bird. I am in silent conversation with the heron. I am deluding myself, perhaps. There is something in the not-quite-silence of the city and the winter acoustic that, together with the proximity of the heron, is transformational, edging towards the sacred. *I said this out loud, the word sacred.* Dream ritual. The fisherman has finished his canal vigil for the night. He spills the contents of his bait bucket on the cobbles and walks away, low whistling. The heron assembles itself and becomes a bird again, instead of a heap of broken umbrellas. It drops down to the cobbles and picks through the scattered bait, selecting pieces of silver herring, swallowing, jerking its gullet. And then, slung low it flies down the canal, beneath a bridge, away into the city, silent phantom. It's beautiful. The city is transformed. And, if only for a moment, so am I.

The man with the movie camera is weaving through the crowd on Damstraat. I watch him. I want to walk into the frame but he either doesn't see me or he doesn't want to film me. I am on my way to the flea market to look for a new overcoat. Damstraat is one of my favourite streets but occasionally there's a bit of hassle – that time a dealer stooped down to frisk my shins to see if I was carrying something, perhaps a stash or a weapon. Sometimes Becks and I pretend to be students and go to the Union café for a cheap supper and a couple of subsidised beers, but on more than one occasion we have been asked to leave because we can't produce ID. Some of the heaviest weed cafés are on this street, in between tourist tat kiosks and cheese shops, but it's the road to the flea market so there are always punks and rockers weaving through the drug dealers and holidaymakers, always a sharp edge. Years later, I discover that the filmmaker I pass is Ed van der Elsken, the famous street photographer, documenter of the underground, maker of *Een fotograaf filmt Amsterdam,* which I watch on YouTube, pausing it occasionally, thinking I might spot myself or Becks or recognise faces in the crowd. The photographer films Amsterdam, the action on the streets. That A'dam mutation of leather-jacketed punks and acid-casualty hippy, Skinheads and Hells Angels, the street hustler pusher vibe, the messed-up cowpoke revenants that look like extras in *McCabe and Mrs Miller.* Elsken hurtles through the morning streets in his military jeep, mapping the concentric circles on film, eyeing up the girls, lurking outside coffee shops, the graffiti covered Court House. Here's a glimpse of TT Fingers sitting in with the Leidseplein All

Stars, hunched beneath his parasol. Here's a glimpse of Harold
the Kangaroo Thornton, self-styled 'Greatest Genius Who Ever
Lived' painting a psychedelic mural on the walls of a marijuana
dive. Street kids mug and flip the finger to the camera. Elsken
frames a scrawled message on a wall: *I'm kicking my habit, I'm
sick as a dog and no one sees my sadness.* The desolate wastes of
Waterlooplein where the Nazis rounded up the Jewish residents
and sent them to concentration camps. The sadness in Elsken's
voice as he rides through the empty void of atrocity. He cannot
bring himself to speak of death. He drives on.

I visit Burco in the yellow box room above the Red Light
laundromat he now shares with Simonette. We sit eating chips and
mayonnaise and talking about Liverpool, Simonette wide-eyed in
wonder at our descriptions of this exotic city she only knows as
the home of The Beatles. Scritti Politti's 'The Sweetest Girl' is
playing, reminding me that Burco always buys his girlfriends a
12-inch single, a token of his undying love. Later, when Burco
stands on a canal bridge and pisses on a tourist boat, I write a
poem about him:

> His crimes were petty –
> Post Office savings account,
> Giro fiddles
> and the false receipt of mail from Poste Restante.
> When sawing locks
> off bicycles,
> he would curse concerned passers-by
> for trying to stop him –
> and he loved to piss
> on tourist boats
> as they passed beneath the Damrak bridge.
> One night, in a restaurant,
> dipping into someone else's cheese fondue
> he explained his theory of delinquency –

'Act like an innocent tourist
and you're home scot free.'
And when he left, I paid the bill
for four complete strangers
who thought the fondue thief had been me.

One day in autumn, Burco calls at Willemsstraat with pockets full of stolen tulip bulbs and we plant them in the courtyard garden. 'This is the perfect crime,' he said. 'We are literally burying the evidence.' When the tulips bloom in April, he's in tears: 'What we're seeing here is the symbolic proof that a life of crime is virtuous,' he announces like a dignitary at a grand opening. The garden is like a pointillist painting, splashed with vibrating dream-flowers. We toast the occasion with space cakes and bottles of Duvel, listening to punk songs on the World Service. When Pete Wylie's new record, *The Story of the Blues*, comes on, we sit in silence, homesick for Liverpool. It's like a signal from a faraway friend, and we want to go home.

On more than one occasion I see a man I recognise from Liverpool, walking down the street, often with a beautiful young woman. We went to the same school, but I never got to know him – I was in the year above him, and in those days a single year was a generation apart. In Eric's club on Mathew Street, he was a face, part of the burgeoning band scene alongside Julian Cope, Pete Wylie, Will Sergeant. Sitting on a bench or outside a pavement café I watch him walking by, but I never say hello. Years later, this man whose name is Paul Simpson of Teardrop Explodes (and later The Wild Swans and Skyray) will become my closest friend, and we will sit in The Grapes in Liverpool talking about our Amsterdam days and wondering how different our lives would have been if I'd only said hello.

Years later, during an artists' residency in Bill Drummond's Curfew Tower in Cushendall, County Antrim, we sit in the writing room like lighthouse keepers, Paul and I, pipe and cigar smoke in the air, peat on the fire, Terry Riley's 'Persian Surgery Dervishes' pulsating. Paul tells stories of Silver Blades Ice Rink; the echo of pop music, the taste of girls' lips. An open window brings us the cacophony of Cushendall at dusk, the rain, drunks roaring on Bridge Street. A sudden panic in the gutters. At the crossroads below, a boy like a bullfighter falls onto the bonnet of a boy-racer's motor. Horns start blaring. A truck pulls a trailer on which, rope tied like Christ on a crucifix, a filth-covered and wild-eyed man is howling, hair full of shit and ashes – Paul and I think we're witnessing some kind of ritual punishment, a pagan sacrifice. The vision carries on as I lie in bed, blood flowing through my neck, heartbeat in the pillow, malarial dreams, fevered agitation: and then a kind of half-death with car horns blaring. *In the night a knife disappears.* Next day, we tell Zippy the Flesher about the scene – Zippy is the Cushendall butcher who looks after the Tower and those staying in it – and he explains it was *just* a stag do.

April in Amsterdam. First crocuses on Museumplein, lilac, orange and purple splashes on the grass, lifting the spirits on the first bright day of the year. Amsterdam in springtime – every year when April comes, I dream of going back there, the crocus is my dream flower. On the way to the Van Gogh Museum through the Rijksmuseum arches, listen to the flute and cello echoing off the walls. The rhythm of the city changing in the morning light. Crocus light beneath the pale blue sky.

Sunday cycling to the coast, to swim – or in my case, sink – in the grey North Sea. On one occasion the sky falls down, the heavy metal weight of the Space Shuttle flying low over Zandvoort, juggernauting in a curve and heading back to England, seemingly pulling the ocean in its wake. Hitching to Utrecht or Rotterdam, crate digging in the flea markets for jazz and blues records, scoring German army motorcycle jackets, and on one wet winter afternoon, first edition Christopher Isherwood books put the idea of moving to Berlin into our heads. Hitching back from Rotterdam in torrential rain, we are dropped off on the hard shoulder of the motorway, and run like chickens through gaps in speeding cars to get to the side that gets us back to Amsterdam, car horns blasting as we slip and slide on greasy tarmac, hearts racing. Back at Willemsstraat, Robicheau has installed a gas heater, cannibalised from a boiler. We take our clothes off and dry them on the heater, sitting wrapped in blankets in clouds of rising steam.

On Queen's Day, 27th April, we load up the bikes with unwanted clothes, trash night gleanings, salvage from scavenger hunts in derelict warehouses, setting up shop on Dam Square on the steps of the National Monument. Dead-mens' suits, a moth-eaten Turkish carpet, splintered guitar, paratrooper boots, mohair jumper, stove-top coffee pot, stolen nail varnish, copper jam pan, bicycle saddles. Queen's Day is like an exploded caravanserai sprawling across the city. A flea market that's taken over the streets like a post-apocalyptic carnival. String quartets, amped-up blues bands, ukulele clowns, oil-drum percussion mutants, pancake sellers, chocolatiers, soup kitchens, stilt-walkers and wire walkers, fortune tellers, pranksters and sleight of hand magicians, hairdressers, puppet masters, madmen, and out on the Dam, moving slowly, a scuba diver swimming through the crowds in slow motion, his flippers slapping on the cobbles. We stand on the monument steps for most of the day, selling the stuff we've dragged here, and when we're done, we drink most of the takings.

I cycle to the tulip fields with Burco to see if we can find a job in the flower factories. We ride through geometry. Straight roads stretching to the horizon, fields like enormous swatches of electric colour. All of Europe's petrol station bouquets are in bloom here and the landscape has the migraine glare of an endless, monotonous Mother's Day. Burco's Moroccan hustle hasn't worked out and so he's now our resident painter and decorator, even nicking paint testers from the HEMA and daubing them on the walls, looking for the perfect pastel hue. As the day wears on, it becomes increasingly obvious that we're unemployable. We bump into people we know from city bars and most of them are addicts or people on the run. We sit in a Portakabin café and Burco bursts out laughing, his broken teeth dripping with hot chocolate. 'It occurs to me that we're not criminal enough to pick tulips,' he says. 'We need to up our criminality.' Years later, in Richard Foster's brilliant book *Flower Factory*, which tells of his time working in this strange territory, I read these words: *Arcadia is packed by a collection of tearaways, addicts, wannabe poets and escapees from all sorts of trouble.* We qualify for all these categories, but no one even says they'll get back to us if there are any vacancies. I wonder if Burco's poncho puts them off. And yet, these days of cycling, looking for jobs, are the happiest I've been, mainly because Burco doesn't give a fuck and every time we get turned down, he's got some kind of slapstick response, like the time he scooped up all the complimentary sweets from a posh hotel reception desk, threw them into the ceiling lights and danced to the *clinkety-clink* of mint imperials cascading into the fake Art Deco lampshades. Or the time he cycled into the foyer at the Hilton demanding to see John and Yoko or at least the bed they occupied.

We never get offered a job.

And round about this time we go to Berlin, Becks and I. To escape the cold, we go to an even colder place for some reason neither of us understand. Everything I know about Berlin comes from books and music. Moths-to-flames tourism, the *cheap holiday in other people's misery* attraction of the Berlin Wall, Cold War fantasies, Bowie and Iggy, the industrial romanticism of Blixa Bargeld's band, Einsturzende Neubauten, Christopher

Isherwood's 1930s-set novels, *Berlin Alexanderplatz* by Alfred Döblin, overdosing on Fassbinder films at the Bluecoat Film Society and cobbling together an idea of Germany from rumours. We get the night train from Amsterdam, white out everywhere, helicopters circling towns in the East and at one point a platoon of soldiers join the train, file down our carriage, kneel in pairs facing each other, rest their heads on the opposite man's shoulder and fall asleep. It's beautiful, childlike, as if we are travelling through a winter dream where tender soldiers rest their sleepy heads and dream of snow. When Becks and I wake up, we're in Berlin Zoo Station and our train is about to depart for Moscow. We grab our bags and run, out into the ice-bound streets of the city, *Christiane F* territory – sex shops and kebab dives shuttered, heroin addicts eyeing us as we huddle into the morning cold, looking for a place to stay, already thinking, *We have made a mistake. Another one.*

We rent a room in Charlottenburg, a high-ceilinged place with blood-red velvet curtains, marble floors and a Lee Miller bathtub in a bathroom where icicles hang from the broken light. We cook soup and noodles on the camping stove. Drink rum. The concierge is a Weimar throwback, Bay Rum fumes coming from his centre-parted hair and waxed tache. He eyes us – quite rightly – with suspicion and polishes the door handles every time we touch them. When we return from our forays into the city, we can only get back in the building when he's ready to let us in. We wait on the doorstep, peering through the glass. We don't let him in our room because we've already pulled the velvet curtains off their rails, two days into our stay.

Even though it's April, Berlin is snowbound and we're completely unprepared for the cold. We build a snowman in the Tiergarten, freezing in our A'dam flea-market dead-men's clothes. On one of the Wall viewing platforms, I watch a man and woman my dad knows back in Liverpool, clearly having an affair, gazing into each other's eyes as if lost in a romantic movie set against the backdrop of Cold War winter. At Checkpoint Charlie the guard confiscates our half bottle of rum, and we walk through the empty streets of the East in search of a bar. The night is drab – I remember it as charcoal daubs, sudden magnesium flares of light as trams rattled through the otherwise silent city. Following a group of men into what looked like a derelict building, we found ourselves in a workers' canteen where we drank beer and schnapps until curfew. It resembled a scene from Alfred Döblin's *Berlin Alexanderplatz* mixed with a Wild West saloon. We had slipped into a secret city of laughter and abandonment. My memory of the tram ride back to Checkpoint Charlie is daubed in noir shadows, expressionist cinematography. When I think of East Berlin I can hardly remember daylight.

In Kreuzberg we drink Turkish coffee, thick and sweet as pudding. Venturing into the SO36 is like walking through a portal back to the squat-zones of Amsterdam, anarcho-punk atmos, broken city. Berlin is collapsing in on itself, civilization is coming to an end. Blixa Bargeld strides through the ruins like an end-times punk prophet. My Guillain-Barré syndrome kicks back in, flashbacks of neurological disintegration. The last things I remember of Berlin are aquarium tanks full of carp in the KaDeWe department store and the tears rolling down my face as I kneel before the tiger cage in the zoo, heartbroken for the beast and for my own feeling that I'm about to die. I wake up in a fever on a broken-down train somewhere in East Germany, Amsterdam bound, going home.

In Willemsstraat the kitchen table is full of food – a wheel of cheese, ham, cured meats, spaghetti, tins of olives and tomatoes, bread, pastries, Swiss chocolate, aubergines, jars of pickles, sambal and cornichon, apples, marshmallows. The cupboards are full of wine and beer – we didn't have cupboards before we left for Berlin but now, mysteriously, we have bright Van Gogh yellow cupboards above and below the sink, cannibalised from a wardrobe. We sit, surrounded by food, completely baffled. It's the jars of sambal that suggest the answer to the mystery: Robicheau. We begin to eat the food and all is explained a few days later when a letter arrives from the Giro Bank – a thousand guilders has been withdrawn from my account; I have twenty-eight days to pay it back. The letter includes a facsimile of my signature on the withdrawal check. It isn't my signature.

I go to Robicheau's and thank him for the food. He's pleased, asks if we like the cupboards, tells me I don't look very well, makes a joke about eating more sambal to make me strong. I ask him about the thousand guilders. He shrugs: 'Of course, it was me, how else would I have paid for all that food?' He says it's OK to steal from the bank, but when I tell him I must pay the money back, he doesn't get it: 'No! No need Jeff... not a problem, the money belongs to the bank!' How did he know how to forge my signature? Before we left for Berlin, he suggested we leave my library card with him to look after and maybe he would use it to get some books out. Given it was Robicheau who encouraged me to join the library in the first place, I suggest to him he'd planned this all along. He's furious, starts shouting about how friends don't say things like this to each other. He grabs me by the collar of my coat and he's going to hit me as his eyes fill with tears. I say, 'If I get into trouble with the law for this I'll go to prison. I'll get deported, don't you understand?' He smiles at me through watery eyes and says he just wanted to make cupboards for us and fill them up with food.

The day after the Robicheau revelation my parents come for a holiday, sleeping on our makeshift bed. Every morning my dad asks if we've got mice and I say no – because as far as I'm concerned, we haven't. My parents love Amsterdam. They walk for hours every day along canals, browse in antique shops and art galleries on Nieuwe Spiegelstraat, gawp in dismay at Red Light hookers, buy wheels of Gouda cheese. Spring has disappeared and the winter's never going to end. I put this down to my psychic disintegration. I describe the lilac, orange and purple crocuses on Museumplein to my mum but when I take her to see them, the hoped-for flames have perished in the cold. We walk on ice in the frozen Markermeer and cycle through floodplains on rickety bicycles. I come home from cleaning the AMRO one evening and my mum is cooking for eight anarcho-squatters huddled on the floor around the heater smoking weed. She either doesn't care, or – according to my dad – she's oblivious to what they're smoking. 'Well, I think your friends are absolutely lovely!' she exclaims when they go off into the night carrying slices of appeltaart wrapped in greaseproof paper, my dad gathering up the ashtray saucers and throwing the spliff stubs in the bin.

One afternoon I leave them in the Van Gogh Museum and go to the Aliens Office on Waterlooplein. I tell the clerk I want to register for residency. I want to go legit. The day before, I'd gone to the police station on Warmoestraat and told them what had happened with the Giro account, the thousand guilders. If I want to make a statement I have to be registered as a resident. Otherwise, I'm fucked. The cop actually said this to me, 'Get registered, otherwise you're fucked,' laughing so much I start laughing too. Naively, I think this is all going to be quite straightforward. But the clerk in the Aliens Office asks for proof that I have legitimate employment and work more than 24 hours a week. I can't guarantee any of this. He stamps my passport. I've got twelve weeks to find a job and if I don't, I'll be escorted to the border. I go to meet Becks and my parents in a café. Becks is looking at me. She knows.

When my parents' holiday is over and we move back into the bedroom – the place is crawling with mice. *Here we go again.* I fill the holes with cement and gravel but they eat their way through it before it dries, and sometimes we see a mouse scuttling through the flat wearing a carapace of concrete.

A few days later, after I work my shift at the AMRO, I get the bus back into town with my friend, the thief, Robicheau. Robicheau likes to drain his bottle and throw it in the canal for target practice. Two or three bottles of flip top Grolsch. Every day the same: we get off the bus after cleaning the AMRO and sit on the wall of the bus station on Marnixstraat, eating paprika crisps and drinking like old timers on the stoop, Robicheau sucking on his pipe and hurling stones at bobbing bottles, as if this was the life, *as if this was it.* But it isn't it. It's nothing. It's the dog-ends of despair. Everyone I knew had come here looking for something – or running away from something – but nobody had found it, and nobody had escaped. Slugging beer from bottles, watching swans on the canal, Robicheau's head shaking, slowly, angry or disturbed by something in his head, something he can't handle. Would Robicheau have opened up more if we shared a language? I can't say for certain, but my feeling is that he lived such a complex life of secrecy, horror and – perhaps – guilt that he would have still kept it all locked in even if I spoke better French or if he spoke better English. What happened in Angola? What happened in the Congo? I wanted to know and didn't want to know. If I knew, I would feel complicit in his deeds. He drains his bottle and throws it into the cut, snatches my bottle out of my hand, throws it in the cut. The bottles bob. Robicheau picks up pieces of gravel and lobs them at the bottles. Target practice. *Dunk, dunk, dunk,* bottles bobbing, half sinking, bobbing back up to the surface. He forms his arms into a shooting position, fires off an invisible air rifle. *Pop! Pop! Pop!* And then he adjusts his aim and 'shoots' the swans. I tell him this is *Niet normaal,* one of his phrases. He jabs his imaginary gun into my chest, pulls the imaginary trigger. 'Niet normaal?' Jabbing. 'Niet normaal?' He shoves me in the chest.

He wants a fight. I won't fight him. He shoves me against the wall and I'm remonstrating with Robicheau about the futility and stupidity of the bottle thing because I can't face talking about the stolen money and my deportation stamp, and he's doing his Belgian shrug, shaking his head and smirking at my righteous indignation when an armoured car rolls into the bus station and positions itself like a roadblock. *This is it. It's happening.* For weeks now there's been tension building up on the streets, and the squatting community has been on a war footing. I say to Robicheau, 'I do not know anything about you. I don't know who you are.' And the air has stopped moving, the city seems to be holding its breath. And I walk away from Robicheau and move towards the Concertgebouw, drawn to the energy of something burning, something dangerous.

The blossoming of latent alternatives. I read this phrase in Geert Mak's book, *Amsterdam,* in which he writes about Philip Slater, the American cultural sociologist's idea that revolutions are not so much a renewal as the reappearance of dormant turmoil. As it dawned on me – dawned on everyone who witnessed the insurrection – the latent alternatives to the surface normality of the city were erupting because nobody listened last time or the time before that. From 1965 onwards, there had been *happenings* centred around the street urchin statue on the Spui. The fact that the statue was a gift to the city from the wealthy owner of a cigarette company really pissed Robert Jasper Grootveld off, raised his countercultural hackles. Queen Beatrix's marriage to an ex-Nazi sent the prankster into a spiral of Big Tobacco/anti-monarchy anarchist revolt, pulling in ideas from Dada, Surrealism and the Situationists – an exhilarating spirit of anarchic disobedience that filtered through the years. Frequently in my years in Amsterdam, there were uprisings – the *shadow government* Kabouters who campaigned for a green, sustainable city using nudity, witchcraft, sex picnics, rituals to bring down skyscrapers, all leading to the elections in 1970 when they won 40,000 votes. The legacy of these antic provocateurs and Kabouters was the Kraken Tactic – the squatting of empty buildings to create new homes in an overcrowded city. You could still feel echoes of this in the 1980s, traces of Paris '68 and the Yippy movement in America. Anti-City protests like Stopera brought attempts at insurrection onto the streets. The building of a new opera house on the sacred ground of Waterlooplein brought marches, riots, bomb scares. The American Embassy was repeatedly picketed in solidarity with the people of El Salvador. The right to shelter, the importance of play, the need for peace were central to the philosophy. And yet parts of the city looked like mediaeval war zones. Squatters armed themselves. Rooftops became arms dumps – fridges and washing machines were stockpiled for bombarding bailiffs and the police. Decaying neighbourhoods were being left to rot by a council intent on demolition and redevelopment. The alliance between community activists and squatters led to community centres, playgrounds for children, a reimagining of the city as a place of possibility. When Hans Kok, a Staatsliedenbuurt squatter, died in police custody from an overdose of methadone, the movement had a martyr. By the time the Lucky Luijk squat was evicted, members of the squatters movement had been training in the dunes and formulating battle plans. Lucky Luijk as a battleground spilled out onto the streets. You could smell the smoke and petrol in the air.

When I walk into Museumplein the cobbles are now missiles. Fumes, clouds of smoke, the hammering of makeshift battle shields and the beating of night-sticks. Cops advancing on gangs of streetfighters, the burning stench of petrol-soaked rags. I go as close as I dare, feel the heat of fire. A tram is burning, weirdly beautiful, engulfed in red and orange flames, black clouds spewing out like demons. In a clearing of smoke I see Bill the Wolf, slowly walking, swinging a leash in his hand, his dog Arpet trotting along at his side. Plum coloured velvet, jaunty cap, a cane, ever the dandy, like a man out for a quiet Sunday stroll. He pulls his neckerchief up over his mouth and nods towards the insurrectionists, as he walks slowly towards the Vondel Park. He's thinking, *Not to believe!*

One afternoon I go to the police station on Warmoestraat and make a statement about the stolen money. I come here straight from Robicheau's flat where we talk about the theft. He tells me I should do the right thing – I should shop him to the police. And then, for the first time I find out his secrets. It all comes pouring out and he tells me about the wars he has fought in as a mercenary, about the wife who left him and the daughter she took with her. He tells me he has killed people on battlefields for money. He tells me that he didn't mean to hurt me, that he loves me, loves Becks and that I am his friend. He starts to cry. I think I'm supposed to hold him. I nearly do. But instead I walk away and leave him there in tears. I walk across the city and make a statement to the police, and the next day they tell me they know Robicheau and he is wanted in two countries. I'm not even surprised. I feel empty. And then, on the Monday market, I see him for the last time. He's walking slowly through the crowds with the Algerians – Hakim, Zuthimalin and Medusa. Our eyes meet, that Robicheau twinkle, the tilt of the head, and then he's gone forever.

Things are spiralling out of control.

I can feel the end of my time in Amsterdam coming when the Maoist Alan Reeve, one of the Staatsliedenbuurt squat agitators, is involved in a shootout with the police in our back garden. This happens on the same day as the second goldfish burial, when Becks accidentally kills a pet fish in a cleaning accident at the house she's been working at as a nanny. I have to find a pet shop, buy a new one and bury the dead one in the mass pet cemetery in our garden. I then go to Bill's to say goodbye. On the stairs there is a dark red, almost black stain the size of a dinner plate. Bill stands on the step above the stain, I stand on the step below, bending down to look at it, to touch it with my finger. It's sticky, like tar. It's blood. *Not to believe!* 'Mondo, he had trouble. He was attacked in the night. The bad guys came, so unfortunate, poor Mondo. He is dead.' Apparently, Mandy the girlfriend witnessed the attack and left in the night, never to be seen again. I tell Bill that I'll come and see him if I'm ever back in Amsterdam. He purses his lips, mimes a kiss, turns and climbs the stairs and he is gone forever from my life.

In some ways the day we leave is a normal day. We walk through the Jordaan streets, to the tram stop, saying hello to neighbours, to the man in the corner shop, to the bicycle repair man. We say, *Hello,* we do not say *Goodbye.* People nod, as if they'll see us tomorrow. This is the chance to change our minds and stay forever but we do not change our minds. We bunk the tram to the edge of the city. And then we're standing on the side of a motorway on the edge of Amsterdam. We're going to Morocco, Becks and me, and when we've been to Morocco, Becks is going to South America, and I am going back to Liverpool to see if I can write. I'm going to be a poet. I'm going to live in Liverpool 8 where poets live, and I'm going to write poems about Amsterdam and Bill the Wolf and Robicheau. On the last night in Amsterdam, I say goodbye to the Night Heron on Herengracht, goodbye to the ragged poet-bird in its poet's overcoat. On the last morning in Amsterdam, I bought Oud Bou a goldfish. We all sat in the courtyard garden – me and Becks, Burco, Oud Bou, Mimi from upstairs; Oud Bou spitting her tobacco juice on the flagstones, cackling and toothless, her sparkling goldfish circling in its bowl.

HERE IN THE DARK THERE ARE HORSES AND
ANGELS AND A BROKEN BIRD IN A SHOEBOX
NEST. Soon it will be dayli... and my
DAD WILL COME HOME FROM TH
FACTORY NIGHTSHIFT. I don
to come home, or rather
come home

REWARD
Arschloch

invisible
the dream of disap
OF DISAPPEARING.
PPEARING. THE DREAM

ITS NOT BECAUSE OF
TO BE INVISIBLE INV
INVISIBLE INVISIBLE
INVISIBLE INVISIBLE
INVISIBLE INVISIBLE INVISIBLE INVISIBLE
INVISIBLE INVISIBLE INVISIBLE INVISIBLE

WILD

WILLS'S CIGARETTES.

DRIFT

His tender heir might bear his memory

Now stand you on the
And many maiden g
Much liker the
So should the li
Which
Thine pen
Neither perceive
Can feed and check
To gen away yourse
And wear
Your
ease,

With means more blessed
held in lease
you were
self's decease.
your sweet form should bear
And (constant stars) in them I
As truth and beauty shall together
If from thyself to store thou wouldst convert
Or fee of thee this I prognosticate

y do
lene
ow one string.

DREAM

When day's oppression is not eas'd by night,
But day by night and night by day oppress'd?

WE DON,T KNO WHAT TO
DO. WE HAVEN,T YET
learned how to travel.
we understand the form
of moving from here
to their, from one place
to another but we don,t
know what to do when we
arrive... It's not how
to do. On the beach,
against a wooden
water I try to sleep
d of the wind and
, huddled in a gully.
range lihts, noises,
st of rising tide,
iced in shadows, scuttle

A HISTORY OF ADVENTURE

WILD TWIN

TWIN

Part Three

The house inside my chest is
empty now – a vacant lot;
the weeds grow wild in there,
and still heart not come back.
Soon the foundations will be swept
away, and underneath the chest's vast
empty skies, only the cries that
echo from afar, of some strange
flapping bird, no longer navigating by a star.

Dorothy Molloy,
'My heart lives in my chest'

Time Machines

In the year my dad was dying I started building time machines. In tobacco tins and cigar tins I curated memories. While my dad slept, I wandered around his house, opening drawers and cupboards, pulling out small objects and arranging them inside the rusty tins. Thimbles, foreign coins, medals, brooches, holiday snaps, acorns, pebbles, seashells, door keys, lucky charms, earrings, lace handkerchiefs, spoons, poems, cigarette and tea cards, the broken heads of dolls, marbles, cufflinks, dried flowers, corks, buttons, chess pieces, teeth. Arranging these objects, glueing them into place inside the tins felt to me to be a kind of ritual magic, or a different way of making a poem, each object echoing and resonating with its neighbouring objects, a rhyming, rhythmic pattern, enhanced by the battered patina of the tin, becoming talismanic, imbued with powers. Portable magic. Tiny museums. Conduits for divine protection, perhaps. By placing fragments of poems alongside the objects – Yeats, Eliot, Edwin Muir, David Gascoyne, David Jones – I imagined I was creating vessels for a kind of primitive chaos magic, each tin in possession of its own atmosphere and narrative. And somehow these vessels would act as time machines, as portals to the past. I was channelling one of my favourite artists, Joseph Cornell, and his 'theatres of the mind' – boxes full of mysterious birds, constellations and childhood toys like aviaries and circuses. And I felt a kinship with Tom Phillips's *A Humument*, his altered intervention into the pages of an old Victorian book. I thought of memory as being *in the present moment*, rather than in the mists of wherever 'The Past' is. I imagined my tiny museums and tobacco tin time machines were living engines of today and tomorrow as much as they were reminders of the past.

And as I've said already, my father's house is a cabinet of curiosities curated by my mother. I sit here in our living room now, in the shadows, looking at the nick-nacks on the shelves and the display cabinet full of ornaments. A magical system of memory. This is where the angels live, a host of tiny angels, grouped in a circle like a white ceramic choir. Filaments of memory, suspended in the room. Holiday snapshots. The time we saw Charles Hawtrey on holiday in Tintagel, skipping down the high street in neckerchief and jaunty Breton cap... the open topped sports car on the same holiday, zipping down a country lane, and Dad telling us the woman in the back street was definitely Olivia de Havilland... Mungo Jerry's *In the Summertime* always on the radio on the holiday in Lyme Regis, and us walking to the beach singing along... The first time we ever saw a hippy on the promenade in Ilfracombe, a bell swinging from a chain attached to his wrist... The caravan holiday in Bigbury-on-Sea, riding the sea tractor to Burgh Island and realising we were in the place where the Dave Clark Five filmed *Catch Us If You Can*... The day trip to Dartmouth, lunch in the Wimpy, watching them filming *The Onedin Line* on the dock, sitting on the next table to Jane Seymour and Anne Stallybrass, Dad like a schoolboy with a crush... The photograph of Dad standing in our half-inflated dinghy on Challaborough Beach, the boat I hardly ever used because I couldn't swim and was frightened of the sea...

A semi-detached in a suburb of Liverpool. I have written about this place before, but avoided mentioning it by name. Maghull. There, I've named it. Sometimes people would get in touch and tell me they'd worked out where it was, asking me why I hadn't named it. I'd reply that I feel ambivalent about the place and part of me has always wished we'd never left the terraced streets of Walton, in the shadow of Goodison Park, Everton's ground. Naming it would have given it more value than I thought it deserved. There is – and always was – something mythic about the old house at 81 Winslow Street, Walton, Liverpool 4. Maghull just didn't have that charisma, that mythic shade. But in the very act of writing my book *Ghost Town,* I realised I had a secret love for the place – this nondescript dormitory town beyond the city limits, the canal and surrounding fields, the River Alt, the psychiatric hospital, the woods, the ruins of the transit camp, the mystery of military tank traps and pillboxes. Without these places, my childhood and teenage years would have been far less strange, less exciting, less dangerous, so much less imagined and imaginary and imaginative. So, when my dad's health began to deteriorate, I began to visit Maghull again, and in 2023 I was there every week, two days and nights, me and my sister Kathryn in the house that was our home when we were young.

So I am sitting in the room where my haphazard journey to Paris began, almost fifty years ago. The day I said goodbye to my parents, the day my dad quietly told me that hitchhiking to Paris was a *silly thing to do.* My dad is now asleep in his living room, in a homecare hospital bed that rattles and sighs as it inflates and deflates to stop him getting bedsores, caged in behind metal safety rails to stop him falling out. Disabled and in constant pain from crippling arthritis, he can no longer walk or even move his legs, is mostly asleep and highly medicated, or awake and mostly silent and seeing visions. He has Alzheimer's. We say the name of this disease as if we know what it means. We don't know what it means until we are in its presence. Alzheimer's is in the atmosphere of this room, and the silence or not-quite-silence of our waiting.

★

I sit and listen to him breathing. In the same way I used to listen for my daughter's breath when she was a baby, now I listen to him as if he is a child, which, at the age of 92, he somehow is. This is the silence, the not-quite-silence I have become used to. The sounds of his body. The hydraulics of the adjustable bed, which also seems to breathe. The noises the house makes as it sighs and leaks and shows its age; the weather, particularly wind and rain on the garden window. The muted ambient music of our days.

There is a Lavinia Greenlaw poem called 'The sea is an edge and an ending':

> My father has lost his way out of the present.
> Something is stopping him leaving, nothing becomes
> the immediate past.
> The act of forgetting used to take time.
> Now it accompanies him through each day
> and the world folds itself up behind his every step.
> What unlocked this emptiness?
> He knows not to ask. He knows now how small he is,
> how small his island, how small his spell.

I read this poem, over and over, trying to unlock its mysteries at the same time as wanting to leave its mysteries intact. Something in the atmosphere of the poem brings me into the strange space of my father's room. We don't know if he understands what is happening to him. *We don't understand what is happening to him.* He is no longer our dad, and yet he is in the body of our dad, albeit a diminished incarnation. Once he was so strong, so tall, so physically powerful, but now he is so small, like a child. His world is reduced to his bed in the living room and for two hours every day his favourite armchair. The room was cold when we first started coming here again. Seventeen years of neglect and grief had left the house feeling lonely: *And the world folds itself up behind his every step...* I can see this happening, his life folding itself up and removing itself from his body, some kind of *unlocked emptiness* as he becomes his own negative.

During lockdown he had fallen and been hospitalised in a ward full of old men with dementia. The gentleness of old men in pyjamas gave the ward a somnambulant atmosphere. Occasionally, this mood was ruptured by some grief or anxiety they could not explain, but most of the time the men sat quietly in their chairs or slept, and their visitors would sit quietly around their beds. And if there were conversations, they were quiet too – the hushed murmuring of comfort words and pauses, the tenderness of wives and grandchildren not quite knowing what to say.

There was a man who sat at a bedside table arranging his biscuits in patterns and poring over crosswords in old magazines. Another man was blind but didn't want people to know – he too was an arranger of pill bottles and Kleenex, placing them on his table with great precision so that he could find them, and so that he could demonstrate to anyone watching that there was nothing wrong with his eyesight. How could there be if he knew *exactly* where his tissues were? Another man was in terrible pain but could never quite explain to nurses where the pain was. His frustration and anguish made him angry, and he was often in tears. I would sit there with my dad, watching these old men, my dad bewildered and frightened. *Why am I here with these old men?* He no longer knew how old he was and couldn't understand why a man as young as he was had been dumped in some kind of hotel with all these geriatrics. When a doctor told my sister and I that Dad almost certainly had Alzheimer's, it wasn't a surprise. We had known it but not named it ever since he failed to recognise our mum in the photograph of the happy day in Amsterdam, the bike ride and the laughter. The photograph is on my desk now as I write. Forty years have passed and yet I can remember the sound of mum's laughter. It pours out of the photograph. My dad couldn't remember even going to Amsterdam, never mind who was doing the laughing.

And then, one day when the radio was on, and the Country and Western songs were playing, there was a moment of such heartbreaking beauty that I will never forget it. I hear it, and see it in my dreams: *Almost heaven, West Virginia, Blue Ridge Mountains, Shenandoah River, Life is old here, older than the trees, Younger than the mountains, growin' like a breeze...* A ward assistant stopped working and, standing in the centre of the room, she gestured with her hand to each old man in turn and one by one, they began to sing: *Country roads, take me home, To the place I belong, West Virginia, mountain man, Take me home, country roads.* Not knowing the words, my dad slowly lifted his hands into the air and slowly swayed them side to side in time to the music, his eyes darting around the room from old man to old man, uncertain what was happening but somehow knowing it was a way for him to belong: *All my memories gather round her, Miner's lady, stranger to blue water, Dark and dusty, painted on the sky, Misty taste of moonshine, teardrop in my eye.* In sweet, perfect harmony, conducted by the ward assistant, the old and fragile men were transformed into a dementia choir and the ward filled up with their beautiful voices singing a song they all knew from somewhere in their lives, retrieved from their folded-away memories. And when the song was over, there was silence. The men sat in their chairs, lay in their beds, knowing somehow that they had been altered, even if only for a fleeting moment, knowing that they had shared something beautiful with each other, that through the power of coming together as a choir they had emerged, for a moment, from their cocoons.

After several weeks in the ward, they tell us that because he's considered to be 'medically fit' – this despite him being unable to walk, his Alzheimer's and prostate cancer – that he's now a

Bed Blocker and he will have to be discharged as soon as they can find a place for him. By 'a place for him' they mean a care home. They have concluded he's not well enough to return home, but paradoxically he's well enough to be a Bed Blocker. My sister and I are given a list of five care homes, and we go and check them out. Damp Victorian houses, exhausted staff, sticky lino, old ladies sleeping slumped in front of televisions, stench of chip fat. We try and explain our father's needs, and everyone says the same thing, *He'll be well cared for here.* My sister Kathryn and I sit in pubs and talk it through. We don't believe he'll be well cared for in any of these places. We've heard about the disgraceful state of the care system in this country, and now we're seeing it. We tell the social worker none of these homes are suitable for our dad. For anyone. The hospital and social services begin to get annoyed. Bed Blocking costs the hospital nearly £300 a day, which amounts to roughly £900 million a year for the NHS – a financial pressure they understandably want to reduce. The pressure is on. They offer us one more chance – we view the home and ask for the weekend to think about it. It's still not good enough for our dad. They give us two days to have our think, but on Monday they want a decision. Then on Sunday the hospital phone my sister and tell her he's in transit – to a care home we haven't agreed to. We hurry to the home and get there shortly after he's arrived. He doesn't know where he is. He doesn't know who these people are. He is scared, and cold, and frightened and he's in tears, sitting in an armchair in a freezing cold bedroom full of shit furniture and a member of staff telling us he's *settling in nicely.* We get him into his pyjamas and put him to bed, propping him up with cushions to stop him falling out. We tell the duty manager he needs a hospital bed, to keep him safe. She tells us he'll be fine. We leave him, he's shaking in fear, we kiss him goodnight, we go home, we cannot sleep. Our sleeplessness is such that we believe we'll never sleep again.

★

On his first night in the care home, he falls. He is injured, a doctor comes to clean and dress his wounds. The care home doesn't tell us. We visit him and see his cuts and feel his fear. He is cold. He's wearing someone else's clothes – tracksuit bottoms, which he would never dream of wearing – and a dirty V-neck jumper. His eyes are like a child's. His own clothes are missing. The wardrobe is full of clothes belonging to the previous tenant. In the bedside cabinet I find the previous tenant's medical notes. We visit every day, and every day he is more frightened. He thinks he is in prison and doesn't understand why, *what crime he has committed?* When the lift breaks, they leave him unattended in his room. He wets himself. When the lift is fixed, they take him downstairs to the lounge where he sits in a circle with the other 'prisoners', in front of the television. Sometimes they play bingo and he sits and looks towards the door, hoping to be rescued. He doesn't know who we are, but he wants us to take him home. *He doesn't know where home is.*

No one will help us, no one will listen. We discover that the hospital discharge form claimed he could walk unattended, that he was capable of rational thought, of making a decision. *He can do none of these things.* He shouts when we are leaving, panics, his eyes fill up with tears. I have never seen him frightened in my life.

We take him home.

The journey in the taxi is such a strange half hour, like taking a geriatric child for a drive for the very first time. He sits in his wheelchair, holding the taxi door handle tightly, stooping forward and watching the world speed past him, his head switching from side to side, his eyes seeing shops and factories as if he's never seen a city before. Occasionally he glances at me, uncertain of who I am, where we're going, what will happen when we get there. I think of him as valuable cargo and hold his hand. When we get back to his house and wheel him into the living room, he sees it for the very first time, even though he's lived here sixty years. This is all we can do for him; this is where he belongs.

Warmth and love, quietude and sleep.

Beyond the room, through the enormous window – the one I broke when we first moved into the house – there is the garden. When our mother was alive the garden was her dominion, nurtured through the seasons, ever changing, like a painting she kept reworking, its changing nature was part of her story, unfolding in her own small corner of the earth. For seventeen years this place has been a lost garden, overgrown, an overspill storage space because the garages and every room in the house are full of furniture and junk. The main garage has collapsed, crushing dressing tables and cabinets. Beneath tattered tarpaulin sheets on the patio there are antique chairs and coffee tables, veneer cracked, swollen with rain, warped and rotting. When it's all cleared away and the grass is cut, the old plants my mum tended start growing back and blooming in the spring. New shrubs are planted, we start putting food out for birds. In his bed, dad watches.

First the starlings come, and wood pigeons and sparrows. Then the robin – our family's spirit bird – and blackbirds. Coal tits, blue tits, long-tailed tits; black caps, goldfinches, greenfinches. The bird feeders are a festival. For two days there is a moorhen, far away from water and lost. And like visitants from a folk tale, two woodpeckers start hanging off the suet-filled coconut shells on the derelict garage wall, bringing a sense of the wild to the semi-detached. Squirrels come, feral cats. Meanwhile, hallucinating on morphine, the old man in the bed sees visions of crows in the living room. He feeds imaginary birds, throwing imaginary bread into the air and calling them to gather around him. I watch this strange, slow motion shadowplay in the dimly lit room. Like a puppet with tangled strings, he reaches out, unsteady hands, pressing his fingertips together and then holding one hand in the air as an invisible sparrow settles on arthritic bones. Time stands still, I hold my breath, and the invisible bird flits away and out into the *real* garden, so believable we watch it fly away and into the ivy at the far end of the lawn. And then, one morning there is a mad panic of birds beyond the window, scattering every which-way, and it seems as if the temperature drops, and the day grows suddenly dark – a sparrowhawk. It drops from heaven, like a missile, leaving a murdered starling in pieces on the grass, as if it has just killed it out of spite, disappearing as quickly as it came, leaving a deathly emptiness. The old man watches the theatre, the murder scene, the place of obscene beauty.

The radio is on, quietly. I listen to pop songs from the 60s and 70s. Dad claims to have no interest in music. When he was a young man he would go to dances – he went to ballroom dancing classes hoping to meet girls. Big band and New Orleans jazz were his thing, Duke Ellington, dancing in the Picton Hall to Mick Mulligan's band with George Melly singing. He can't remember any of this. He can't remember being a beautiful dancer. I turn the volume up for the glam rock, for T.Rex and Slade and Bowie, remembering when my sister Val and I brought records home from NEMS and played them on the downstairs stereo, teased by Dad for choosing them. Sometimes there'd be a memory song like Roger Whittaker's *New World in the Morning* or Bob Lind's *Elusive Butterfly*, the strange beauty of these songs disturbing the atmosphere, the lyrics of *New World*, strangely apt. *I met a man who had a dream he had since he was twenty. I met that man when he was eighty-one. He said too many people just stand and wait up til the morning, don't they know tomorrow never comes.*

★

In primary school, every playtime I watched The Supremes. They would sing *Baby Love* three times, finger clicking, hands pulling kisses from the air, hips tilting slightly, wiggling like mermaids. Of course, we weren't watching Diana, Florence and Mary. We were watching a Polish girl called Lynne Kuszczak and her classmates Rita and Debs. Half the school would gather on the tarmac, waiting while the girls pinned their hair up into beehives, and then we'd stand there, heads bobbing, whispering the words and dancing to the finger clicks as Lynne led her girls through her song of broken-hearted loss and desire. As far as I was concerned, they *were* The Supremes until I saw the real group on *Ready, Steady Go*.

Pop music *is* memory. Sometimes I would go to the far corner of the playing field with a boy who had a pocket transistor radio, and we'd lie on our backs, sucking on clover flowers and listening to Radio Caroline. Once a week I'd go to NEMS on Central Square in Maghull, usually with my sister Val, and she'd buy the latest Tamla Motown single, or we'd go to Woolworths and buy Upsetters LPs for a quid. Back home in her bedroom she'd work out her dance moves and memorise the words of *Baby I Need Your Loving*, spinning the record over and over again on the Dansette – the yearning loneliness, *Empty nights echo your name*, sung by my 12-year-old sister, dancing on linoleum. Later, when I was old enough, I'd go to the Empire to see The Temptations and The Four Tops, in awe of these immaculate Americans and their night-time dramas of desire and sorrow. Standing on Lime Street after seeing the Jackson 5, feeling the electricity of the crowd surging, molten, exhilarated, hoping for a glimpse of Michael in the Holiday Inn, I had a sudden, wired-to-the-constellations feeling that the city had somehow been changed by the presence of angels and not only was *I* altered by the experience, but the city was too. And then, moving on a few years, Marc Bolan at the Stadium, the sheet metal screams of hundreds of teenage girls, my sister's tears, her hand clutching her heart; David Bowie's Ziggy Stardust show at the Empire, the stench of sweat and piss; the seemingly annual Roxy Music shows and the beauty of their dandy followers gathering in the Legs of Man before the show; the proto-punk sonic assault of The Sensational Alex Harvey Band – *And remember, boys and girls, when freedom comes along... don't piss in the water supply...* Doctor Feelgood at the Stadium – Lee Brilleaux's sky blue suit just about recognisable as a suit beneath the stains. Oh, the thrill, the wonder, the sweet ecstasy, the sense of danger, the voyages of discovery, the tears. The soul map of the city, the sonic cartography of Liverpool is so vividly inked into my imagination that I can hear music coming from venues that no longer exist. Turn the dog-leg corner of Sweeting Street and I can hear Deaf School performing *Second Honeymoon* fifty years ago, the moody, cigarette-smoke fug of the cellar welling up in my mind so clearly that I can still remember the words on the tip of my tongue as I rehearsed, and how I tried and failed to ask that French girl out on a date, succumbing to the music instead, falling into the bittersweet atmosphere of the song. If I walk up Bixteth Street (why anyone would want to walk up that soul-void street is another matter) and pause at the spot where the Stadium once stood, I swear I can hear Hawkwind's Space Ritual sending seismic tremors through the office blocks, or see myself and my friends standing in the street in tangled knots of fire hoses on the night Cockney Rebel had to stop playing because the building was on fire. The pavements and the architecture are ghost radios, if you listen. I listen. I can hear *Diamond Dogs* in Beaver Radio on Whitechapel and I can see myself waiting for the bus in Skelhorne Street with the record under my arm. I can see myself taping songs off Top of the Pops, hear the muffled warp of *Resurrection Shuffle* and *Tokoloshe Man* when I listen to the cassette player I got for Christmas. Memories of semi-detached houses in the suburbs, my friends and I in darkened bedrooms, the thrill of taking the record out of its sleeve, the needle drop, the first ever time we'd hear Lou Reed's *Transformer,* Bowie's *Aladdin Sane,* listening to *Marquee Moon* on the radio in the dark. Then, later, Vic Godard,

Pere Ubu, Magazine, Talking Heads, The Raincoats, Popol Vuh, onwards into endless explorations.

Alone in my room, listening again and again to Minnie Riperton singing *Les Fleurs*, trying to fathom its miraculous beauty. I can hear the sweet poetry of scratched pop records, the laughter of my sister and her friends dancing on her sixtieth birthday to *Tracy* by The Cufflinks, *Sugar, Sugar* by The Archies, and Edison Lighthouse's *Love Grows (Where My Rosemary Goes)*, the songs they once danced to at the school lunchtime disco, still dancing together in a circle, dream-dancing like time travellers, backwards through their lives. And now that Val's gone, when I think of her, that's where I see my sister, dancing and happy in the back room of a pub in Ormskirk, dancing to bubblegum pop four years before she died.

Rain pours through a hole in the garage roof, onto the Rosedale Electric organ and a battered acoustic guitar. Rain music falling on instruments covered in spider webs and mildew, Theremin wind blowing through the ruins. Sometimes in the night, a piece of broken furniture in the garage gives up the ghost, disintegrates beneath the weight of the broken garage roof, a metaphor for the experience we're living through. A three-legged black cat moves into the ruins, occasionally coming into the house and curling up on the old man's blankets. When the two woodpeckers start visiting the garden, we all know how the folktale is going to end.

I meet my friend, the musician Benjamin Duvall, and we talk about *Lodge,* an improvised piece of music he made with his group Ex-Easter Island Head, a haunted farewell to their shared communal home and rehearsal space. I've been listening to this piece of music over and over, sinking into its shadows and becoming possessed with its emotional ghosts. In the spaces between harmonium drones and melancholy upright piano, I can hear birdsong and weather, and moving through the music there are phantom memories of the nursing home that the house used to be, its long-departed residents seemingly haunting the recording's air. With Jonathan Hering and Benjamin Fair, his fellow musicians and housemates, Benjamin improvised a leaving ritual. FM/AM radio static and guitars with vibration speakers placed on the guitar's body. There is rainfall, the elements are drawn into the room, and the music is freighted with a sense of home, of departure, and loss. It could almost be the music of my father's house.

Benjamin collects discarded plastic bottles and pop cans on the walk down to the river. He cuts into the tin and plastic, turning rubbish into wind instruments, then places them on the railings separating the water treatment works from the promenade. Weather music, haunted calliope, storm breathing. Dog walkers and sunset strollers listen to the accidental orchestra. I live near the river and sometimes I walk down to the promenade, or to the seventeen Scots Pine trees on the adjacent wasteland. I watch the sunsets in the enormous sky and try and remember them and put them in collages and acrylic paintings. Dad's garden window, eight miles from my house, looks out on the same enormity. When the setting sun paints the sky in violets and charcoal and egg yolk yellow, we watch the Canada geese fly across the vast, endless skeins of noise. The sky is broadcasting sound and visions of memory and my attempts to collage and paint what I – and the old man – are seeing is a kind of field recording. When Benjamin records the weather music, he is capturing abstract space, the memory elemental.

In *this* world, the apparent real world, my dad has forgotten that he used to be a junk man, an 'antiques dealer'. We watch antiques programmes on afternoon television, and he is *appalled* by the antics of the presenters and the *load of rubbish* they keep buying in auction rooms, 'Why would anyone want to waste their lives in a place like that?' He looks away, disgusted with the very thing he spent half his life doing. But in his dementia world, he believes we're in a warehouse or an auction room, and that I am a teenage boy. He points to furniture in the room and tells me it's high time we sold that piece and maybe I should move it to the front where we'd stand a better chance of selling it. The display cabinet of curiosities curated by my mother is full of ornaments and 'best China'. The drawers are full of teaspoons, sewing hooks, cigarette holders, wedding cake decorations, caddy spoons, corkscrews. Sometimes, he asks if he can have a look through the drawers and we sit together as he takes each object in his hands and examines it, taking pleasure in the silver or copper piece, turning it over in his hand and nodding his head in pleasure. 'That's a lovely sugar spoon! It's probably worth at least ten pounds.' He is like a child, lost in wonder – and then he's a junk man again, an antiques dealer, just for a fleeting moment, enough to make me cry.

How did we get here, to these days where my dad is an old man who can't remember his life? I tell his home carers who he is, the things he used to do. They love him. He is always so polite, even when he's in pain, when he swears – he never used to swear – he apologises, always says *Thank you*, impeccably well-mannered. He makes them laugh, flirts with them, tells them fragments of stories, which fade away into silence. We look at wedding photos – Mum and Dad, full of light and life, walking down the aisle, cutting the wedding cake (the bottle of HP Sauce on the table next to the cake always makes us laugh). He was handsome. She was beautiful. They met when they were twelve. The story goes: he wrote three love letters to three different girls and asked all three to meet him at the gates after school, not expecting them all to turn up. When the three girls arrived and realised what he'd done, they chased him down the street. Mum was the fastest runner, so she caught him and kept him forever.

★

They spent their lives together, and when she died he was alone, lonely. I have never seen a man become his own ghost but this is what happened to him, to his soul. And then, when my sister died, he was *dismantled,* hollowed out. The ghost of a ghost.

Atmosphere. I am looking for something I can compare it to, for something comparable to the mood of this experience, for something that will help me make sense of this atmospheric weather. In the room, I see the ghost of my mother, she is there in the drab, faded wallpaper and the threadbare carpet. I look at Francesca Woodman's strange and beautiful photographs – Francesca fading into peeling wallpaper and broken mirrors, into the disintegrating plaster crumbling from the walls of empty rooms. The room we are in is damaged by rain and fire. The ghost of my mother comes in the form of birds. When rainwater pours in through the hole in the hallway ceiling, the house is full of weather. There is a photograph of Francesca, stooped behind a broken umbrella against a backdrop of parched plants and crockery, an uncanny apparition. In his bed, my father is a spectral vapour – a kind of ghost weather rather than a man – and you can hear his throat, his body, his murmured questioning of his own predicament. He wants to die; he tells us often. The sound of the kettle boiling, and a plate of broken biscuits is a small domestic detail of normality in the strangeness of the night.

When I worked with the musician Philip Jeck on a project called *The Ballad of Ray and Julie,* he created a sound atmosphere out of scratched records and faulty equipment. Old 45s, flexidiscs, minidisc recorders, wires, plugboards – things I didn't understand were all brought into the service of summoning distorted beauty, seemingly from the air around him as he hunched over his table of electrical research materials like an alchemist in a primitive laboratory. The project was a commemoration of two metal chairs in a vacant lot on Liverpool's London Road, a gaping space between a barber's shop and a pub frequented by right wing thugs. The artists Alan Dunn and Brigitte Jurack placed the chairs there as a piece of public sculpture, a place to pause in the mayhem of the city, inspired by a scrawled graffito saying RAY + JULIE on the back wall of the gap. I had written a sequence of texts about Ray and Julie. We didn't know who they were, and we still don't, but the idea of the graffiti becoming a pair of chairs for Ray and Julie to sit on – as if in their own living room – became a London Road secret history, a half-remembered love story of two souls who had found a place in the world, in a wound in the city's skin. Philip Jeck's musical séance seemed to contain Ray and Julie's voices. The texts I wrote were love poems exchanged between the lovers, and the project had an atmosphere – that word again – of romantic longing, of yearning for the unreachable. When I listen to the music, I can hear the city. I can hear Liverpool, and I can hear and see myself as a child, walking down London Road after going to the Odeon cinema with my parents, holding my dad's hand as we wait to cross at the lights. When Philip Jeck died, I listened to the Ray and Julie music because I was too ill to go to the funeral. When I sit in the darkened room in my dad's house, I can hear loneliness and love and the broken songs of ghosts.

Memory then, remembering, here, in the present day. The distorted memory is better than – is now *realer* than – the actual event. The memory of the Prudential man's fingerless gloves in Winslow Street sixty years ago only matters because the image is still with me, glimmering. The memory of the man trying to catch his canary in a shoebox only matters because I can still see the canary, even if the bird is now a cartoon. The memory of the coins spinning through the air and hitting the office window is still rattling, but now it's in slow motion, like a samizdat film clip.

★

Here is an Amsterdam memory that might not even have happened. It's impossible. In a way, it's inconsequential. In another way, it's stayed with me forever as if folded in my wallet long ago, and I keep finding it whenever it's time to pay the bill. Crossing a bridge on a morning walk, I see Bill the Wolf, slowly walking his dog, Arpet, leash twisted in his hands, messy cigarette balanced on his lip. He doesn't see me. He tidies up his magenta bob, tilts his chin coquettishly, a beautiful apparition fading into his own reverie. He slowly shakes his head, a hint of rueful regret or bemusement. I wonder what he is thinking: he is thinking, *Not to believe...*

This glimpse of Bill happened nearly forty years after we lived with him, when he must have been long dead. The glimpse is a hallucination. It happened on a visit to Amsterdam for my sixtieth birthday, with partner Amy and my daughter Pearl. We also went to the house on Willemsstraat, on a ritual memory walk. And I couldn't find the entrance, couldn't remember which door led into the covered alley. As I stood there on the pavement trying to work it out, a window opened on the first floor of the house behind me, and a man called down: 'You are looking for the house you used to live in?' I looked up and nodded, yes. He pointed his cigarette towards the door and nodded: 'This is your old house.' We went in, we stood in the courtyard garden, the place of goldfish burial, place of rabbit and budgerigar internment. I looked into the kitchen window of the flat I used to live in, and I remembered the day of moving in, of the bombardment of vegetables and pans. Oud Bou was long gone. The garden was full of roses. Nothing had changed and everything had changed, and I could not comprehend the passing of the years.

In Paris in 2023, again with Amy and Pearl, I go to Rue Git-le-Coeur looking for the hotel I stayed in all those years ago. In the archway leading off Place Saint-Michel there's a homeless woman

sleeping surrounded by lit candles in bottles. I stop at the place
I expect the hotel to be but there is no hotel. I look for the Beat
Hotel, but it's not there either. I turn a corner and find it but it's
not where it is in my memory, and the hotel I stayed in doesn't
exist. We go to Shakespeare & Company; there's a winding queue,
snaking around the corner. It seems the shop has become a tourist
attraction because it features in a TV series. No one wants to
read the books inside the shop, they just want to visit a television
location. Because of the heightened security measures resulting
from the Israel-Palestine war, there are armed cops everywhere
and the constant blare of sirens, riot vans speeding through the
streets, cops with guns guarding the entrances to museums.
We stand in front of the burned-out shell of Notre Dame. We
are evacuated from the Louvre because there is a bomb scare –
hundreds of people herded along Rue de Rivoli by cops with
guns, cops with guns everywhere. And yet, it's beautiful. Autumn
light, the river in the evening, the city lit like diamonds as we gaze
out from the top of the Eiffel Tower. Going to the bench in the
Luxembourg Gardens where I used to sit in the 1970s, and sitting
there remembering. The pilgrimage to Beckett's grave, to Serge
Gainsbourg's grave – the first austere, the second like a shit-heap
bed. In the hotel room, I think of my dad in his room faraway.
In the distance between two rooms, in the space between my dad
and I, I can hear him breathing.

Not so long ago while I was visiting my dad, I showed him the
Amsterdam photograph again. I watched him, peering at – into
– the photograph, and I could see his mind working, struggling
to remember who the woman was. Mum and Dad on the bicycle,
Dad at the handlebars, Mum on the pannier rack, Dutch style,
wobbling along the towpath on the north bank of the IJ. Once
again I could hear the laughter in the moment, pouring out of
the photograph, a happy day always to be remembered until the
day you forget. That was the moment he said, 'She looks like

a really nice lady.' As I write this I can see the memory of that pause, when I realised he didn't know who the woman was. I can see me, glancing sideways to check whether he's joking. I feel the pause.

This pause happened not long after Val died. Her death was like the end of everything that mattered, and this pause was like a pause within a larger pause. I do not have an exact metaphor to show you the impact of it, the perfect metaphor eludes me, so I'll just say that my sister's death – *the death* – opened up a fault line, a fracture, and we fell inside it. Everything that happened from that point on was aftermath, was trauma. And I wonder if the realisation that my dad couldn't remember my mother, was also the moment when I knew that he had fallen into the fracture. The moment when the pause button was pressed on his memory, because remembering was so painful that it was easier to forget.

After Mum died in 2002, my dad hadn't wanted visitors to the house. I didn't go home for seventeen years. My younger sister Kathryn had visited a few times and he'd reluctantly let her in. She reported back: things had 'got out of hand'. In 2019, Dad fell in the street and spent a few weeks in a hospital frailty ward; I finally went home and saw it all for myself. How he'd spent the years since Mum's death filling the house with furniture, every single room in the house, from floor to ceiling, even the stairs. And ornaments, household goods, pots and pans, bric-a-brac. Because he was a secondhand goods dealer and spent his days in auction rooms, it wasn't difficult to source all this stuff. Effectively, he had turned the family home into a storage warehouse, but he had lost control and was bringing more stuff in than he could possibly sell. What used to be the living room was now wall to wall wardrobes, sideboards, cupboards, apart from a narrow passageway winding its way through the furniture to an armchair, an extension lead and a kettle in the middle of the room. The ceiling was black with soot from a blaze when a stack of paperback books stacked next to the gas fire had caught, adding to the weight of sadness.

Cardboard boxes full of glass and crockery were stacked up in between cupboards, and every single piece of furniture was full of junk. And, on top of all this, the house itself was falling to pieces. Drainpipes and gutters had fallen off, cracks had appeared in the brickwork, water had poured through the roof into the hallway which no longer had a ceiling. The house itself was in mourning for my mother, as was our dad who – although unable to articulate it – had seemingly been so lonely and bereft in the empty spaces she once filled, that he had instinctively, with a broken heart, filled the vacuum with whatever he could lay his hands on. The house was now a storage mausoleum full of brown furniture and cooking pots and trifle bowls.

One of the things that struck me about all this junk was that every single object was a repository of someone else's memory, because it had got to the auction rooms from the house clearances of dead peoples' property. The house was a museum of grief and loss and abandonment, and our dad was the curator. Memory, memories everywhere, museum, library, archive. As much as I was appalled, I was also aware of a deep, resonating poetry in all this. It was terrible and beautiful at the same time.

We began to clear the rooms. Skips were hired, journeys were made to the tip and recycling centre, boxes were filled with stuff to sell at car boot sales. And during this time, I had started to fall to pieces, physically and mentally. My left hand seized up completely, swelled up like inflated sausages. Unimaginable pain. My doctor referred me to a rheumatologist whose first question was, 'Have you experienced any kind of trauma recently?' When I asked if he meant physical or emotional he replied, 'Either'. I told him about my sister's death, and how we gathered around her bed when she was dying, and how she held my hand tightly as if she were sending me a signal from her morphine coma, and how her breathing got louder as we wrapped our arms around her and then she breathed her final breath... and then how a single tear rolled down her cheek and I caught it on my fingertip and put the salt water to the tip of my tongue, and it was as if the single teardrop was her saying goodbye. And how I swallowed her last tear. The consultant was a kind man and he listened quietly. It was such a relief to tell him. It was already a memory and it shone like a teardrop. The teardrop. And as terrible as the memory was, it was also strangely beautiful. And it was – and is – the most vivid memory and it will never go away.

Illness moved into my mind and body, and I began to close down. Medication had such an effect on me that, combined with the illness, I couldn't move, couldn't think. Cognitive diminishment meant I couldn't read more than a page of a book without feeling exhausted. Every afternoon I had to sleep, sometimes for two or three hours. Once, I walked several miles a day, but now I couldn't walk for more than half an hour. I found myself in hospital with a heart condition. Almost every week I had a hospital appointment for one condition or another. There was a science fiction angiogram, a hallucinated orbit in which I experienced nightmares even though I was awake. It had the fevered atmosphere of my Guillain-Barré syndrome flashbacks. The procedure only lasted for an hour but it seemed to last for days as I orbited the moon. I was already on compassionate leave from my teaching post when I was diagnosed with another illness, illness piling on top of illness. I retired early, retreated into silence. The list kept on growing: two types of arthritis, coronary-artery disease, respiratory problems, osteoporosis, skin cancer. Soon I was taking 150 pills a week for my various diseases. The genetic neurological disease that killed my sister hung over me like a shadow. And I couldn't write. I had to pull out of the series of radio dramas I was writing on jazz musicians because I couldn't even focus on their music, let alone their lives. My mind worked so slowly, so clumsily, that sometimes I couldn't speak. Trauma and memory had occupied the spaces inside me. It occurred to me that I was like a human version of my dad's house, filling up with trauma and memory in the same way as his house filled up with *memory furniture* and the possessions of departed strangers. Perhaps in the folktale version of this story, all of this was birthed by the salt of my sister's final tear.

I sleep in my parents' bedroom, I sleep in my parents' bed, I hardly ever sleep. In the wardrobe, Mum's christening gown, faded delicate lace, and in a metal cashbox, one hundred letters from Becks in Par Avion envelopes from her time living in Amsterdam, before we went to live there together. I cannot bear to read them. Time is overlapping. Dad calls out in the night, a childlike *Heelp*, as if checking he's not alone. My sister Kathryn sleeps on the sofa in the room and when she gets up to care for him, he's sometimes angry, sometimes sad and lost. She soothes him back to sleep. In the dark of my parents' bedroom, I have the feeling we are drifting in a shadow orbit, a dimmed solar system of breathing and awaiting the inevitable. In the sombre mid-watches of the night, we are waiting for his death. But in the morning, it is one of the woodpeckers that is dead on the patio, left there by the sparrowhawk or the three-legged cat, a portent of what's to come, an occult symbol of death's shadow.

The mantle clock is ticking. He wants to tell the story of the clock, the wedding gift from Alfred Shennan, Mum's boss, visionary architect of cinemas and synagogues. But the story disappears, and his words fade away into a silent disappointment as he shrugs, feeling lost, the memory beyond his reach. He's always had a repertoire of stories but now he cannot find them. He tries to tell the one about the Everton footballers upsetting Mum when we lived opposite Goodison Park, and how he stormed into the changing room demanding an apology and threatening to *kick their ruddy shins in.* He cannot find the story in his heart. Every day he asks me why I haven't combed my hair: 'Have you lost your comb?' He stares at the carcinoma and solar keratoses on my forehead – he doesn't ask what they are and I don't explain. But we talk about my useless left hand. Because he's spent his life working with his hands, he cannot comprehend how I can cope. I don't tell him that I *can't* cope: I just smile and tell him I'm okay and he looks at his own hands. He talks about *skyjumpertrains* and asks, 'How's your chunk of wax?' He enjoys our laughter at his Stanley Unwin phrases, as if his tongue has lost control of the things he wants to say. He tells us with great authority that he is looked after by between two and four nurses. When one of his carers asks him who I am, he replies: 'I think he's my nephew... actually, I think he's my deputy nephew.' He also asks us to help him find his legs, and tells us he sees two people watching him from the garden – they came into the house while we were out. Uncanny revenants, perhaps, visions of something to come. He says it doesn't matter when he tries to ask a question and we don't understand. His face is telling us *it matters very much...*

Our daughter Pearl's final year A-Level Photography project is a cabinet of curiosities – an installation that replicates his living room and moments in his life. She borrows objects, ornaments, the wedding cake angels and birds, mementos and souvenirs. She makes Joseph Cornell boxes and places the objects inside them against collaged backgrounds of photographs of him in various stages of his childhood, youth, marriage and old age. She takes photos of him in his armchair and films him as he tells – or attempts to tell – the old stories. He can't finish the stories. You can almost see the thoughts fading away, watch them reversing into his mind through his pale blue eyes. Into silence. If you walk through Pearl's installation you get a sense of who he was and of what he means to her. He doesn't know she's made him the centre of her final year photography project, but he can tell how much he means to her. The pieces of an old man's life have been arranged by his granddaughter, in a schoolroom, in a memory bank of love.

I fill tiny glass storage jars with seeds from the garden, with petals. I place them in a time machine – a State Express Cigarette tin containing marbles, a pair of cufflinks and an ornamental mustard spoon. I cut the words, *A Grief Ago* from a Dylan Thomas poem in a compendium of verse and glue the scrap of paper into the tin. A portable altar, a way of travelling into some kind of sacred imaginary. I try to capture the memories before they disappear into the wallpaper, into the watercolours of cottages and bridges in imaginary villages, into the photographs of weddings he can't even remember attending. The Green Lantern is in this room, the Silver Surfer, Doctor Strange, Patrick McGoohan, Barbara Stanwyck, Adrian Street. My dad asleep in his hospital bed in the living room of the house he's lived in for sixty years. He doesn't know it's his house. He thinks it's a strange hotel. He asks: 'What time are we going home?'

I am listening to Gavin Bryars's *The Sinking of the Titanic*. It makes me feel as if I'm falling through dark waters. If you go down to the river by my house just after sunset, you can sometimes hear the exhaled breath of a solitary seal – or the *imagined* exhaled breath, in the aqueous acoustic. Close your eyes, listen. Marconi transmissions through time, onward into eternity, the hymn of a lingering sonar signal in the sea of memory. Trying to avoid closure. To keep it going, continuing, into the erasure, the infinite. 'I don't know what's going to happen,' Dad says quietly. We leave it there, hanging in the birdsong and not-quite-silence, where the memories are, lost and forever. As always, we are living in the ghost town...

★

We look at the photograph again. Mum and Dad in Amsterdam, 1983. They're in their fifties, dad's hair still dark, mum's hair curly, probably a perm. Mum is still on the back rack, Dad holding onto the handlebars. Laughing. Laughing on the north side of the IJ, a factory behind them, a dismal day. The photograph is muted – that washed out Instamatic tone that makes everyone look old fashioned and ill. But there is no illness in the event in the image, there is only joy. He gazes into the photograph. His hand hovers close to the image, almost reaching into it. And then he says, quietly, 'I think that lady might have been my wife.'

I go home and sleep and suddenly wake up and reach for my phone to check the time. It's 4.30 in the morning. And as I look at the phone it starts to ring and it's my sister. He's dead.

I get dressed, get in an Uber, and when I get to his house I walk into the room, hesitate, turn to the bed. My sister is sitting on the sofa in silence. I touch my father's hands and he is cold.

Trauma doesn't always come as pain. After my sister Val died, I felt as if her death was inside me, like a heavy metal occupying my body. After my dad died, I felt haunted by absence. And yet, the absence had a presence. My body felt like there was subsidence inside me, as if I were a building that was tilting and sinking into the earth. In both instances I ceased to feel human, and yet paradoxically I was more human than ever because grief is all consuming. The altered state of grief is physical, material, and it made me feel as if I were sinking into the ground.

Remembering the day I left this room I get a flashback to the hitching trip to Paris. Remembering black ice, cracks like lightning. Remembering the wooden porch of a supermarket, like a hillbilly shack. The mildew smell of boots. A cluster of white snail shells in the weep hole of a brick. Crushed pop and seltzer cans, click-clacking underneath the tires of passing trucks. Small, illumined images, lodged in memory for some ungraspable reason. Why these, rather than *important things?* Then it was an ongoing moment, now it is an accumulation of the half-forgotten but ever present, the misremembered but eternal, akin to dream. I hold my father's hand.

I read George Melly's *Scouse Mouse,* immersed in inner space. You can feel the rooms crowding in on you, can almost touch the heavy furniture and ornaments in the rooms of his childhood. It's overwhelming. I go to Ivanhoe Road and stand outside George's number 22, imagining the weight of memory resonating in those shrouded rooms. This is what is happening in my dad's room – the resonating memories in objects and furniture and spoons.

Amy and I go to look at Andrew Cranston paintings in the Hepworth Wakefield and I am moved to tears. It is as if he has painted *my* inner space, as if each encaustic wax vision painted on the cover of an old book is a magic lantern, an illumination of a resonating moment. Sometimes he removes paint from the canvas with household bleach – by taking away rather than putting on. The fragility of the disappearing reminds me of the atmosphere of my father's room, where memory becomes *not* remembering, like life being blown away by abstract weather. In his book *Never A Joiner*, Cranston quotes a poem by R. S. Thomas: Silting the veins of that sick man / I left stranded upon the vast / And lonely shore of his bleak bed. Cranston's painting *The Strand*, of a sleeper, a dreamer, reminds me of my dad. When he writes of his painting *Clots*, he says: *Go against the light – contre-jour – but don't succumb to silhouette. That's too far.* It's beautiful and I begin to cry.

In the twenty-eight days that pass between the day he dies and the day of his funeral, I make twenty-eight small collages, like prayer cards made from pages torn from old books I find in my old bedroom. Simple, almost blank images, perforated and punctured, burned. I don't really know what else to do because at this point I can't find any words. The paper in the collages is fragile. When it rips, I leave the rips. When the fire burns the paper too much, I let it burn almost to dust.

On the day we bury Dad's ashes in the crematorium woods, there are daffodils and crocuses emerging in the pale spring afternoon. The grey ash pours from a copper canister into the black earth where my sister Val's ashes are buried, where my mother's dust is buried. We do not have a ritual. We haven't prepared any words.

We go, my sister Kathryn and I, to my dad's house and begin to do 'the death admin', look through paperwork, decide to sell the house, decide *not* to sell the house. The presence of his absence. The three-legged cat that used to visit dad appears at the garden door, meowing as if it's asking where we've been.

Owl is here, memory bird, the white-feathered blackbird in a shoe box, the wounded sparrow. Rumpelstiltskin creeping in the shadows, Halloween apples bobbing in a bowl. Childhood magic, storybook wonder, that night when Peter Pan appeared out of the wallpaper as Mum, hushed with wonder, read the book, flying around the ceiling light. The casserole dish full of tadpoles. The day we left this room, water spilling from the bowl, carrying froglets to the brook and setting them free, tears in our eyes. The naïve watercolours hanging on the walls, pale landscapes painted by a neighbour. The Sunday hymns. Mum's voice clear as a bell, brightening the room, embarrassing us kids even though we knew it was beautiful.

All these things are happening in this room, forever. Complicated things are in this room, the mysteries of memory and death, of not-quite death but almost. This is what this room is. This is what this house is. All my life I have restlessly been looking for a home, for a room. And it was here all along.

Acknowledgements

In the last year of his life my dad would often ask what I was writing about and I would reply, 'I'm writing about you, Dad...' This always amused him – why would anyone want to write a book about him? And who would want to read it? But here it is, sadly too late for him to hold in his hands. My sister Kathryn, ever heroic, gave up so much to look after him in his final years and we went through a lot together, the three of us. Part Three of this book is the closest I could get to capturing our lives in his last year. Love to you, Kathryn. Thanks to everyone at Little Toller, Gracie, Adrian, Jon and Graham, and to Sarah Hughes and Tabitha Pelly. We got there in the end! Thanks to the Young, Petricca and Collins families, Auntie Margaret, and Joan Bond. To John Buscombe and all the other Buscombes. Friends, collaborators, good people – Horatio Clare, Paul Simpson, Maria Barrett, David Morrissey, Mike Badger, Bert Byron, John Montgomery, David Lewis, Joe McKechnie, Simon Moreton, Richard Cabut, Davina Quinlivan, Benjamin Duvall, Demelza Kooij, Cathy Cole, Frank Cottrell Boyce, John Canning Yates, Mick Ord, Penny Layden, Jo Pocock, Jill Heslop, Mersey Wylie and Daniel Thorne, Liz and Tom from Atticus, Alan O'Hare, Dave Haslam, Nick Ellis, Lizzie Nunnery and Vidar Norheim, Martin Heslop and Lindsay Rodden. Andrew Lees, David Hayden, Anthony Quinn, Paula Byrne. Old friends Hugh Weldon, Phil Jeffers, Mark and Richard Blanchard. Special thanks to Nina and Will at Rough Trade Books. Andy, John and Nicky at Backlisted. James Quail and everyone at Dorothy. Grant McPhee and everyone involved in 'Revolutionary Spirit: The Pool of Life' especially Peter O'Halligan the Dream Merchant. All of the people mentioned here in one way or another kept me going through the last few years of ill-health, and the illness and death of my dear dad. Since I retired from teaching at LJMU in 2020, lots of my former students have kept in touch and kept me laughing. A big hello and thanks then to Mathew Thomas Smith, Madelaine Kinsella, Joe Turner, Dan Dobinson, Genevieve Glynn-Reeves, Elsa Williams, and many more, too numerous to mention. And a special hello and thanks to Catherine Morris and everyone involved in the Gerard Manley Hopkins Lecture series at Liverpool Hope University. This book is dedicated to all of the above and more and to the lost souls of Wild Twin, wherever they are. Always look up!

Jeff Young
Liverpool, April 2024

Oliver Rackham Library
THE ASH TREE
ANCIENT WOODS OF THE HELFORD RIVER
ANCIENT WOODS OF SOUTH-EAST WALES

Richard Mabey Library
NATURE CURE
THE UNOFFICIAL COUNTRYSIDE
BEECHCOMBINGS
GILBERT WHITE: A BIOGRAPHY

Nature Classics
THROUGH THE WOODS *H. E. Bates*
WANDERERS IN THE NEW FOREST *Juliette de Baïracli Levy*
MEN AND THE FIELDS *Adrian Bell*
THE ALLOTMENT *David Crouch & Colin Ward*
ISLAND YEARS, ISLAND FARM *Frank Fraser Darling*
AN ENGLISH FARMHOUSE *Geoffrey Grigson*
THE MAKING OF THE ENGLISH LANDSCAPE *W. G. Hoskins*
A SHEPHERD'S LIFE *W. H. Hudson*
WILD LIFE IN A SOUTHERN COUNTY *Richard Jefferies*
FOUR HEDGES *Clare Leighton*
DREAM ISLAND *R. M. Lockley*
RING OF BRIGHT WATER *Gavin Maxwell*
COPSFORD *Walter Murray*
THE FAT OF THE LAND *John Seymour*
IN PURSUIT OF SPRING *Edward Thomas*
THE NATURAL HISTORY OF SELBORNE *Gilbert White*

Field Notes & Monographs
AUROCHS AND AUKS *John Burnside*
ORISON FOR A CURLEW *Horatio Clare*
SOMETHING OF HIS ART: WALKING WITH J. S. BACH *Horatio Clare*
BROTHER.DO.YOU.LOVE.ME *Manni and Reuben Coe*
HERBACEOUS *Paul Evans*
THE SCREAMING SKY *Charles Foster*
THE TREE *John Fowles*
TIME AND PLACE *Alexandra Harris*
DIARY OF A YOUNG NATURALIST *Dara McAnulty*
THE LONG FIELD *Pamela Petro*
SHALIMAR *Davina Quinlivan*
ELOWEN *William Henry Searle*
SNOW *Marcus Sedgwick*
WATER AND SKY, RIDGE AND FURROW *Neil Sentance*
BLACK APPLES OF GOWER *Iain Sinclair*
ON SILBURY HILL *Adam Thorpe*
GHOST TOWN: A LIVERPOOL SHADOWPLAY *Jeff Young*

Anthology & Biography
ARBOREAL *Adrian Cooper*
MY HOUSE OF SKY: THE LIFE OF J. A. BAKER *Hetty Saunders*
NO MATTER HOW MANY SKIES HAVE FALLEN *Ken Worpole*
GOING TO GROUND *Jon Woolcott*

Little Toller Books

w. littletoller.co.uk E. books@littletoller.co.uk

DREAM